**PRESENTS**

BASS SECRETS

Where Today's Bass Stylists Get to the Bottom Line

compiled by John Stix

48 *Bass Secrets* Columns by
Billy Sheehan
Stu Hamm
Tony Franklin
Randy Coven

from the pages of *guitar* magazine

ISBN 1-57560-219-9

Visit Cherry Lane Music online at
www.cherrylane.com

♦

Music Engraving and Layout
Staccato Media Group

Book Packager & Cover Design
Dancing Planet MediaWorks™

CHERRY LANE
MUSIC COMPANY

INTRODUCTION

~

The date was May 2, 1983. That was the day my co-Editor-In-Chief, Bruce Pollock, and I started work on *Guitar for the Practicing Musician*. We set out to create a magazine devoted to all aspects of rock guitar playing. We wanted our readers to experience the synergy of what happened when the world's finest players harnessed the power of an electric guitar and pumped it through a heart full of soul (and a Marshall stack). We did this in pictures and posters that reflected the excitement of making music. We did this with words that explored the guitar's role in the creative process. And we did it with music. That was the key. Our original ads showed a torn photo of Eddie Van Halen and proclaimed, "Without music you're only getting half the picture!"

Never before had a magazine included complete transcriptions of songs designed for the guitarist. The idea was simple: if guitarists want to read about their favorite players, they'll want to play their music as well. We weren't just talking about guitar arrangements—we went for mirror-like transcriptions. It took awhile to get it right, but in our "first anniversary" issue we published 21 pages of "Sultans of Swing," just as Dire Straits played it.

Everything in the magazine was to be exciting and useful. We chose the voice of the guitarist to carry the message. Our writers each had his own style, his own approach. But overall we knew that, just like our transcriptions, it was the voice of the guitarist speaking directly to the reader that gave the magazine its impact. The truth is, if I tell you to prepare for a performance by washing your hands in warm water, that's preaching; when Steve Morse tells you, it's Gospel. The messenger counts.

Now, if the guitar transcriptions were rare prior to *Guitar*, bass transcriptions were non-existent. We believed most guitarists reading the magazine would also be playing in a band. So why not invite the ignored bass-playing audience along for the ride? We could only make more friends and build a larger readership by including transcribed bass lines of the songs we put in the magazine.

As long as we were courting bass players, it made sense to devote a column to the inner workings of the bottom line. To this end we invited a series of bassists to share their insights on how they saw the instrument working in the context of the band, the song, the melody, the rhythm, the time, and so on. Just like "Guitar Secrets," "Bass Secrets" was designed to present short, self-contained nuggets of immediately useful information.

Our first columnist almost single-handedly changed the way rock bass was played in the '80s. Billy Sheehan was often called "The Eddie Van Halen of the bass," because of his lead-like style and extensive use of tapping and harmonics. Starting with his band Talas, followed by his work with David Lee Roth and Mr. Big, Billy Sheehan took rock bass playing out of the shadows and into the spotlight. Billy passed the column onto Randy Coven, a Berklee schooled melodic fusion fan, whose lab band, Morning Thunder, included guitarist Steve Vai. Randy also worked with Brian Setzer, Al Pitrelli in CPR, and Leslie West in Mountain. Randy knew his theory and his wang bar. Next up was Stu Hamm, renowned for his work with Joe Satriani and his amazing solo performances. His calling card was humor and spunk rolled up in awesome technique. The "Bass Secrets" torch was then passed to Tony Franklin, known for his sympathetic work with guitarists such as Jimmy Page (The Firm), John Sykes (Blue Murder), Marty Friedman, Tony MacAlpine, and Gary Hoey.

What you have before you are four master classes made up of mini-lessons, each of which may help you to become a better listener, player, and musician. With talent, luck, and persistence, who knows, you may be an author in the next compilation of "Bass Secrets."

John Stix

—*John Stix*
Founding Editor
Guitar Magazine

CONTENTS

ABOUT THE AUTHORS

~

Billy Sheehan

Billy Sheehan is a consummate musician who has changed the way bass guitar is perceived and played. Billy rose to cult status with his band Talas, and achieved international fame with David Lee Roth in the late '80s. In 1989 Billy formed Mr. Big, who had a Number One single with "To Be With You" in addition to selling over six million albums worldwide. The public responded to Billy's trademark style by voting him Best Bassist numerous times in *Guitar for the Practicing Musician* and *Guitar Player* magazine. Billy continues to record and perform with Mr. Big, as well as his cutting-edge instrumental band, Niacin, a bass/drum/organ trio.

Ever-dedicated to the future of music, Billy has a scholarship in his name awarded annually at the Musician's Institute, and he gives bass clinics around the world to share his knowledge and experience with aspiring musicians.

Stuart Hamm

I first became seriously interested in the bass around 1972, when I was growing up in Champaign, Illinois. I was a twelve-year-old geek who played flute in marching band and was prone to wearing embroidered bell-bottoms and brown, fringed leather vests (hey, now I'd be cool wearing that!) and whose idea of cool was Danny Bonaduce from the Partridge Family. Then one day, while atop the monkey bars at Eisner Park, I saw a band setting up on the tennis courts, and not only did the bassist have an orange plush speaker cabinet, he also had a white curly cord for his bass! This was too much for me, so I got a bass for Christmas and soon started playing in the school jazz band. I went to Berklee College of Music in Boston in 1978, where I first met Steve Vai and heard Jaco for the first time—as well as lots of talented local players like Jeff Berlin, Tim Landers, Wayne Pedziwater, Tim Archibald, Baron Brown, and Victor Bailey. After kicking around for a while I ended up in California on the floor of Steve Vai's studio to work on *Flex-Able*. Through that association I landed a record deal with Relativity and then met Joe Satriani when he played on some tracks on my *Radio Free Albemuth*. The summer of 1999 finds me awaiting the release of my new signature bass from Fender and trying to fit in a variety of recording projects around my real job: changing about a dozen diapers a day! That's my story and I'm sticking to it.

Tony Franklin

Tony Franklin—Englishman, fretless bassist, multi-instrumentalist, vocalist, and songwriter. Tony introduced the fretless bass to rock 'n' roll in 1985 with The Firm's catchy hit "Radioactive." Though Tony was the youngster amidst a truly legendary lineup, he was already a seasoned musician, having played regularly on stage since the age of six.

His musical journey led him to work with some of the best in the business, including The Firm, Whitesnake, David Gilmour, Kate Bush, Blue Murder, Steve Lukather, Eric Burdon, and many more.

Tony has also recorded his first solo album, handling the production, songwriting, bass (electric and upright), guitars, keyboards, vocals, and string arrangements himself, showing there are many more strings to Tony Franklin's (bass) bow. . . .

Randy Coven

After releasing three solo albums—*Funk Me Tender*, *Sammy Says Ouch*, and *CPR*—Randy Coven toured with Leslie West's Mountain throughout Europe and the United States, off and on for seven years. During this time Randy also recorded three albums with Holy Mother, a very heavy heavy metal band in Europe, and still found time to produce and play on independent albums by Witness, Frog Daiquiri, and Maddog. Randy has also recorded with Leslie West on *As Phat as it Gets*, as well as working on the fourth Holy Mother album.

A native of Great Neck, New York, Randy was privileged to have Jeff Berlin as a neighbor and mentor. Jeff gave Randy guidance and inspiration to continue his life-long love of the bass. Though Randy took music seriously and played in numerous bands while in high school, it was at Berklee College of Music that he began to make his mark. While at Berklee, Randy met Steve Vai; the two quickly became friends and played in a band called Morning Thunder. Of course this wasn't the last guitar master Randy would play with. Randy has also played and recorded with Brian Setzer, Steve Morse, Jeff Watson, Alan Holdsworth, Larry Coryell, Zakk Wylde, Vivian Campbell, Al Pitrelli, Jack Wild, and Blues Saraceno.

Randy took the Bass Secrets torch from Billy Sheehan and held it for a five years—a *Guitar* magazine record!

PATTERNS ON THE NECK

by Billy Sheehan
May 1985

A lot of players, myself included, play by envisioning patterns on the neck. When it comes to major scales there are only three patterns that I use, and everything that I do with major scales is a variation of one of these patterns. Generally, your fingers are in a position to cover four frets, with one fret for each finger. With Pattern One you extend your reach to five frets on one string, but extending it to six or seven frets remains impractical. Using three notes, with no more of a stretch than five frets per string, you come up with three patterns.

Pattern 1 is a series of whole steps. In the key of C major you start on the low E string with the note F on the 1st fret. Play this with your index finger (1). The next note, G, is played on the 3rd fret with your middle finger (2) and the last note, A, is on the 5th fret, played by your pinkie (4). The B, C, and D notes on the A string, 2nd, 3rd and 5th frets respectively, are also played with fingers 1, 2 and 4. This is Pattern 2, made up of a half step (1 fret) followed by a whole step (2 frets).

Repeat Pattern 2 on the D string for notes E, F, and G. Pattern 3 uses your index, ring (3) and pinkie in the 2nd, 4th and 5th frets to get the notes A, B, and C (Ex. 1).

Ex. 1

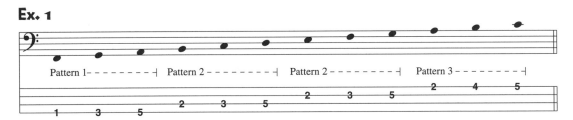

So Pattern 3 is a whole step followed by a half step. You won't be using these patterns verbatim in your bass lines all the time, but you will be using variations of them. They are excellent for making up exercises. If you can do these three patterns in every conceivable variation—ascending, descending, starting in the middle and so on you'll then want to do two notes in combinations.

Here's an easy one-string exercise. Just play the outer notes on each string. It's F to A on frets 1 and 5 on the E string. Then it's frets 2 and 5 on the A, D and G strings (Ex. 2).

Ex. 2

Now let's try Ex. 3, a two string combination. Play the G on the E string 3rd fret and B on the 2nd fret A string with fingers 2 and 1 respectively. Pluck them together and go to the A note 5th fret on the E string with finger 4, and the C on the 3rd fret A string with finger 3. Now pluck this combo. Just take this two part riff down one string and do both parts exactly the same, right down to the fingerings. The last part of this exercise moves what you've just played down another string. However, the final two notes are to be plucked a bit differently. After simultaneously plucking the F and A notes on the D and G strings, you pluck G on the 5th fret D string with finger 4, and a B on the 4th fret G string with finger 3 (Ex. 3).

Ex. 3

You may find the stretch between your ring finger and pinkie a bit much at first, so just take the whole exercise up the fretboard until you feel comfortable. Remember, these ideas are just points to start with. Experiment to make them your own.

RIGHT-HAND SLIDING

by Billy Sheehan
June 1985

This month I'd like to talk about what I call my right-hand sliding technique. Tim Bogert of the Vanilla Fudge used this technique on "You Keep Me Hangin' On" and that's what got me started using my fingers instead of a pick. For this riff the left hand remains stable while the picking hand ascends and slides up the strings. In Ex. 1, your fretting hand, the index finger is on the 7th fret, A string, the ring finger frets the 9th fret, D string and the pinkie frets the 9th fret G string. On the picking hand, the index finger strikes the D string, to ascend to the G string, which is struck by the middle finger, which then slides up across all three strings. It should flow easily when you play it quickly. You can do it with a pick, but not with the same smoothness.

I hear Iron Maiden's Steve Harris doing a similar riff. The fingering stays the same in the fretting hand. The variation starts with the first note on the 7th fret D string. Fret this by barring your first finger on the A and D strings at the 7th fret. After striking the first note, hammer-on to the 9th fret D string and continue the riff as explained above. After finishing the slide, strike the A string again, hitting it twice in a row. Then repeat the riff starting with the hammer on (Ex. 2).

Ex. 1

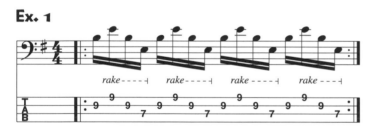

Ex. 2

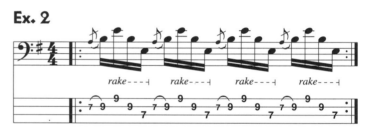

Here is a Stanley Clarke-like various Ex. 3, which reminds me of something I heard on the Romantic Warrior album. The notes in this riff are all parts of a descending C major scale. I think descending scales lend themselves more to finger style players. But the first time I said that, a friend and I were watching guitarist Paco De Lucia, and as soon as I made the statement, he did this unbelievable ascending scale and I felt like an idiot. But let's do this descending scale anyway. Start with your index finger on the 5th fret on the G string. Then go from the 7th to 5th fret on the D string, then the A string. The root C is played on the 8th fret E string. The picking or sliding in this case is done two notes to a finger, starting with your middle finger and alternating with your index. So it goes middle, middle, index, index, etc. This also works as part of a minor scale (Ex. 4). In that case the riff would start on the same note (C) on the 5th fret G string, but the repeated frets on the D and A strings would be from the 6th to the 5th, with the low C note remaining on the 8th fret of the E.

Ex. 3

Ex. 4

SOUNDS

by Billy Sheehan
July 1985

Let's do some right-hand tapping that brings out harmonics. Fret the D and G strings at the 7th fret, then, with your right hand tap both strings simultaneously 2, 3, 4, 5, 7 or 12 frets away. (See Ex. 1.) The placement of your tapping fingers is important. Remember to tap on the fret itself and not in the fret, as you might do with regular right-hand tapping. The tap should hit the strings and fret wire and bounce off completely. Your hand should be loose, like a drumstick on a skin. You can also tap above the neck as well; you just have to find the right places. On a P-style bass one place for tapping could be on the forward edge of the bridge pickup, where the string meets the pickup. The edge of the G and D string pickup should give you an octave harmonic to the fretted notes on the 7th fret. You can start at the bridge and go right up the neck and find tapped harmonics. Tapping the frets or above them, on open strings, sounds a bit like a flanger. I use a variation of this to start the tune "High Speed" on Ice. In my right hand, I use a pick because it sounds more percussive. With my left hand, I start at the nut of the A string and slide up in time, just barely touching the string. I use my finger over the neck instead of the normal fingering position. When you wrap your hand under the neck your fingers curve. When you go over the neck they are straight and you can reverse bend them. The reason for doing this when you want harmonics is that if your finger is curved, too much skin can hit the string.

Here's another fun sound with which to experiment. I got this from the sounds that come just before Greg Lake's guitar solo in "Take a Pebble" on the first ELP album. The notes are open A string, D string, 2nd fret and G string, 4th fret. What you have to do is scrape up the strings with your fingernail. The riff goes from string to string like this: A, D, G, D. Emerson did this by scraping the piano strings with a feather. I got this together because I'm so used to playing in a three-piece band, where you have to mimic things all the time. Try it yourself and see what you can come up with on the bass.

~~~~~

Ex. 1

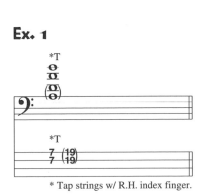

* Tap strings w/ R.H. index finger.

THE PIANO TECHNIQUE

by Billy Sheehan
August 1985

When you find yourself having to pedal one note for a period of time, you may want to spice it up with some piano techniques on the bass! We've got four strings, so let's use them. We'll work with the note G. Hit the low G with your index finger on the 3rd fret of the E string. I use my pinkie for the octave above that on the D string, 5th fret. You've got the same positions in another spot on the neck, the 12th fret, G string, which I tap with my right hand ring finger and the 10th fret, A string, which I play with my index finger (also the right hand). Start off with the ring finger hand. Then go to the index finger on the same hand, followed by the first finger and pinkie on the left hand. (Ex. 1.)

Ex. 1

On this one you're going to want to concentrate a lot on the strength of your right hand and its position. You want to tap in the same spot every time. You should hold your instrument clinched to your body. Use your elbow to hold it in. You don't want your bass moving around too much.

For an even more interesting sound, keep your left hand where it is and experiment with moving the right hand around the fingerboard. For example, when I say the 12th and 10th frets, that means those frets should be played in the G and then A string respectively. Move to the 11th and 9th frets. It's a little dissonant, but it resolves in the next move, which is down a whole step to frets 9 and 7. Go down another whole step to frets 7 and 5. Take it back to the original position of 12 and 10 and follow through to the 14th and 12th frets and 16th and 14th. Keep going to the 17th and 15th frets and lastly the 19th and 17th frets. (Ex. 2.) If you're tired of pedaling 8th notes behind the lead guitarist, give him a jolt of this technique. You may want to experiment by keeping your right hand position frozen in place and let the left hand wander. Have fun.

Ex. 2

HAND POSITIONS

~~~

by Billy Sheehan
September 1985

One of my biggest secrets is that I consistently hit the strings in the same spot. Where you pluck or hit the string makes a big difference in the sound you get. Ross Valory, from Journey, sounds like he plays very close to the bridge, as does Jaco Pastorius. They get a very fast, sharp, percussive and wooden sound that cuts through easily.

The average bass player plays in the middle of the neck, like Tim Bogert. I think that's why the Precision Bass style is so popular—you tend to stick your thumb somewhere, like on a pickup. You need that grip so you have an opposite thumb to pull toward. The bassiest sound is close to the neck, like on those old Yardbirds records.

I don't play the strings, I play the pickup. I want a consistent spot for my fingers to touch and the strings just get in the way. If I were not playing the pickup my fingers would overshoot and undershoot. This way, as I hit the pickup, the string hits the exact spot on my finger every time.

The theory comes from standup bass players. They play on the neck and the strings get in the way. Stanley Clarke plays up high on the bass because he was traditionally a string bass player, so he had that technique. When you see him play the electric, his hand is always clinched up tight to his body, mimicking what he would do on a standup bass. The point of this is consistency and smoothness.

I saw John Entwistle on MTV and I noticed his fingers were all over the place. I was surprised at his inconsistency. His left-hand technique was all over the place, whereas my fingers barely move. I think this makes him work a lot harder than he has to. He doesn't need to refine his technique, but if you're not a legend yet you may want to get the most from your efforts. I'm talking about getting the most movement from the least motion. I see many bass players who take their fretting fingers way off the neck. I only lift them up enough for the skin to clear the string. Any more than that and I'm wasting time getting them back down again. This simple idea should improve your speed and smoothness of playing.

~~~

CLASSICAL RIFFS

by Billy Sheehan
October 1985

Here's a good classical sounding riff that you can use to help develop your hammering and pull-offs. It's especially nice for your pinkie. We'll use the open D string as a drone along with the 11th fret G string. Pluck them together with your thumb and first finger. As the D string is ringing, hammer with your second finger on the 12th fret and then with your pinkie on the 14th fret. Continue this motion by pulling off your pinkie back to the 12th and then 11th frets. Repeat this exact sequence going up to the D and A strings, with the A as your drone (Ex. 1).

Ex. 1

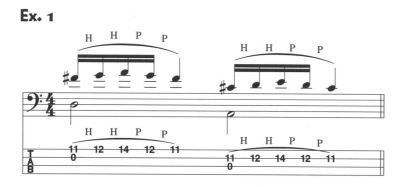

Now place your second finger on the D string 10th fret and your first finger on the 9th fret G string. Again pluck the two of them together and hammer with your third finger and pinkie on the 11th then 12th frets respectively, and then continue on with pull-offs until you've reached your original position. Now move this whole thing up one string to the A and D strings, and let A be the drone while you hammer and pull on the D string (Ex. 2).

Ex. 2

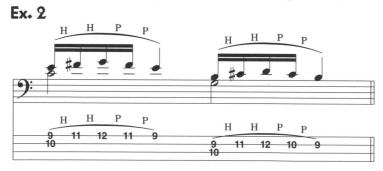

BASS PHILOSOPHY

~~~~

by Billy Sheehan
November 1985

I'd like to share a bit of bass philosophy that is slowly creeping into the world of rock music. It seems everyone is guitar crazy. While the bass and drums just do their jobs, it's all up to the guitarist to add flavor and color. Even when you record, first they get the bass and drum sounds and then they spend the rest of the time with the vocals, guitars and everything else. But when you play a lot of notes on the bass, people say look, he's playing lead bass. WRONG! That's because the only place they've heard a lot of notes on a guitar has been on a six string. I've actually heard a rock musician listening to a sax player blowing his brains out say, "Look, he's playing lead sax." Just because the only place you've heard a lot of notes is on the guitar doesn't mean that's the only instrument that plays a lot of notes. How about the piano, trumpet and saxophone for starters?

People aren't used to hearing the bass play a lot of notes. There's a lead guitar backlash against bass players and drummers who play a lot of notes or get too much attention. I've seen it a lot in guitarists who come to see Talas. Most guitarists are used to having a bass player play soft and supportive. When they hear a lot of notes from the bass, it gets in their way. Talas has a guitarist who is more of a rhythm player and my drummer and I play a lot of notes.

Listen to the Vanilla Fudge or Cream's classic *Crossroads*. Jack Bruce is burnin' all over the place and so are Eric Clapton and Ginger Baker. There was magic that happened there that never happened with any of those three guys in any other band.

The point is that a guitarist has to be less egotistical and more of a group, team player in order for a band to play like that. Now we've got guitarists who just solo their asses off and nobody even knows who else is in the band. Yngwie Malmsteen is an amazing player, an incredible soloist, but everyone else is just a backup for him. I don't know if he's a team player who says, "I'll throw the ball. You run over and catch it while I block for you." You never see the rhythm section of Judas Priest in the magazines. They are one of the best and tightest sections in any rock band around. How about the bassist for AC/DC? I don't even know his name, but I know Angus Young. Yet the guy is great at holding super-heavy roots. The bass players of yesterday were there to hold the guitarist on their shoulders, and they did an incredible job.

The bassist of today is coming into his own, and players are discovering you can play more notes and get away with it. I endure a lot of flack from people because I play a lot of notes. Today's rock guitarists should work with us instead of getting worried about someone else taking notes away from them.

In jazz they play tons of notes on the bass. It takes more time and effort to make that magic happen, but it's the magic of playing in a group. Instead of worrying about lead bass, guitarists should worry more about being competent within the framework of their band.

Bassists Ray Brown and Ron Carter play their asses off, moving all over the place, and you can hear what everybody is doing and it all works together. This philosophy which works to bring out the best in a jazz band is slowly getting into rock. The point isn't to make everyone into a jazz bassist, but that rock bassists are now playing more than just the root and 5th of a chord. Steve Harris writes the songs in Iron Maiden and makes things happen with the bass. Guitarists shouldn't get upset about this; they should capitalize on it. Rather than worry about having somebody move around underneath them, they should move with them like Jack, Eric and Ginger did.

STRETCHING EXERCISE

by Billy Sheehan
December 1985

Naturally, most right handed players tend to have weaker left hands. To me, when my hands are more equal in strength, they work better together. Strength requires tedious boring and painful exercises. Sounds like fun, hey? Here's one: Take your widest useful stretch. By useful I mean one you would actually use when you play, not just to scare other players. For me, that's usually four frets between the index finger and the pinkie. Let's do this as low on the neck as possible, as shown below. Play the first fret (F note) on the E string with your index finger and the fifth fret (A note) with your pinkie. Play these notes one following the other and then move down to the A string with the notes Bb and D played on the first and fifth frets respectively. Go on to the D and then the G string and come back up by string to the E string. Play hard and don't stop till you feel a little pain. Push it as far as you can. I push it to blood, sweat and tears. This move will stretch you out real good and is an excellent warm up before further practice.

Ex. 1

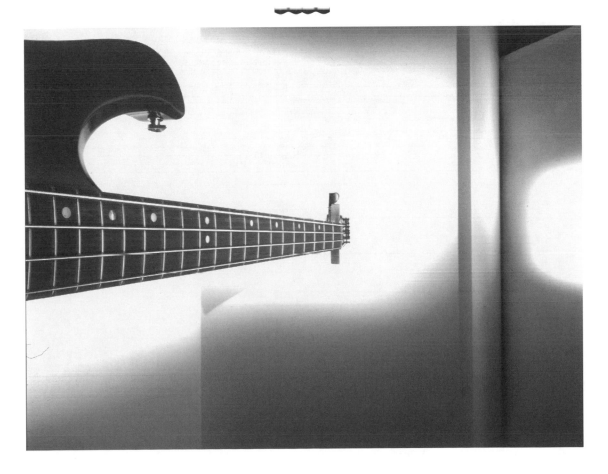

BROKEN CHORDS—MALMSTEEN ON THE BASS

by Billy Sheehan
February 1986

When my old group, Talas, toured with Rising Force, I got to see Yngwie play close up and live for 20 nights in a row. We even had a few mind blowing jams together, and had a great time with a lot of notes. Yngwie was nothing short of incredible and a huge inspiration. Bassists can learn from many sources besides other bassists, and I learned a lot from watching this maniac scorch up and down his guitar.

He does one thing he calls "Broken Chords," which are arpeggiatated chords that split and continue up the neck and over a one-and-a-half to two-octave range. Because a bass has only four strings, it's good to know how these are done, as it will extend your range. Yngwie does these at ridiculous speeds, so when you hear him do it don't get discouraged! An adaptation for bass done on a simple C major chord looks like this: Start with your second finger on the 8th fret of the E string (C) and follow with the first finger on the 7th fret, A string (E). Then slide the first finger to the 10th fret, A string (G) and barre the same finger to the 10th fret, D string (C), fourth finger to 14th fret, D string (E) and follow with the first finger on the 12th fret, G string (G). Lastly, stretch the pinkie up to the 17th fret G string (C) while holding your first finger in place on the 12th fret. Now pull off to the 12th fret, G string and go back down the chord by reversing the order of the notes you've just played.

You can vary this idea infinitely by adding and subtracting notes, doing all kinds of arpeggios and fingerings. Try tapping the last note of the passage with the first finger of your right hand. It should be played with a triplet rhythm with the accent on one. If you want to try this with a minor chord just make all the E notes into E♭'s and leave the rest as is.

Ex. 1

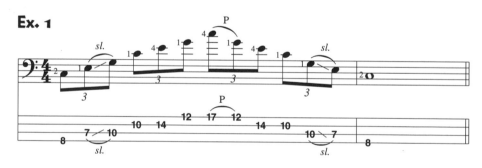

A "MEAN STREET" TAP

by Billy Sheehan
April 1986

Some people have equated me with Eddie Van Halen, which I consider an honor. I've also read letters in *Guitar* where people say I must have copied from Van Halen. The fact is, when Eddie Van Halen came out doing his tapping, I had already been doing it, as had a lot of other people. Eddie does it in his own amazing way and he did single-handedly change the course of rock 'n' roll. One side of his brilliance shines on the intro to the song "Mean Streets." When Talas was touring with him, I watched him for 38 nights in a row. He did this intro in his guitar solo before they released the *Fair Warning* album. I remember that I couldn't figure it out for anything. Eddie finally showed me that the secret to the technique was where I wasn't even looking. It's a tap between the right and left hands. If you tap your thighs, pretending to play drums, you're close, only you'd have to tap the underside of one thigh and the top of the other to equate how it would be on the guitar or bass. The key is that the left hand, at time, is completely independent.

Here's an example similar to "Mean Streets." Since your right hand is generally faster, you play doubles there. Use the index finger of your right hand on the 12th fret octave of the E string. You want to bounce that note twice and follow it with a tap by your index finger, left hand, on the A note (5th fret, E string). The move is bounce, bounce, hit, or right, right, left. You're getting the bass drum effect of doing flutter doubles with your right hand. Try this move in the frets I've indicated, on the E string, and follow it up with the same move on the A and then D string. Continue the lick on the D string with a tap on the 9th fret, followed by a pull-off back to the 5th and a hammer onto the 7th fret.

It's a weird technique because Eddie uses his fingers independently on the left hand in conjunction with the bounces he's doing with the right. It's like playing with drum sticks, only your left hand has two or three sticks that work independently. The amazing thing about this technique is that unless you're a drummer you wouldn't naturally think about it. It's a classic that kind of slipped by people. This was so far out that almost nobody would have thought of it, except Eddie.

Ex. 1

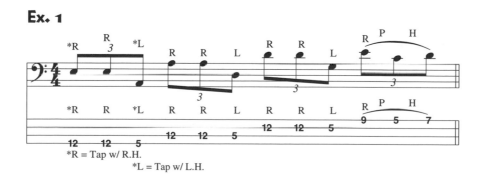

*R = Tap w/ R.H.
*L = Tap w/ L.H.

CHORDS

by Billy Sheehan
June 1986

While your guitarist and drummer are flailing away at the end of a song, it's good, once in a while, to set an example by holding things together rather than flying all over. Try just pounding out a big chord for the ending. In E minor, which most heavy metal seems to be played in, I hit a big open chord like open Em, second finger on the second fret of the A string (B), third finger on the second fret D string (E) and the open G. It's simple. Now with your picking hand put your index finger and thumb together as if you were holding a pick. As you stroke down, the top of your fingernail hits and on the upstroke the top of your thumbnail hits. Try all kinds of open and barre chords. Try an E5 chord with the open-E string, your first finger on the 7th fret, A string (E octave), your third finger on the 9th fret, D string (B) and your fourth finger on the 9th fret, G string (E octave). How about the open-E string with a first finger barre on the 2nd fret of the A and D strings (B and E) and your fourth finger on the 4th fret of the G string (B)? These chords are made up of stacked fifths and octaves, which work well as bass chords played loudly. They are also good whether used in a major or a minor context.

Ex. 1

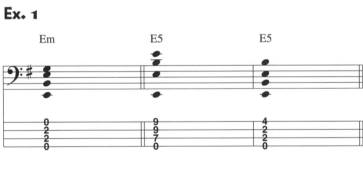

FINGERPICKING

by Randy Coven
January 1989

The reason for exploring fingerpicking is to develop independent movement in your pick-ing thumb and first and second fingers. Fingerpicking is most often used for classical, folk and blues guitar playing. Let's try it on the bass. To start, place your right hand in the middle spot between where the neck ends and the bridge. This will give you a nice mellow sound. Ex. 1 is a simple classical sounding piece to get you started. It might be a little awkward at first, but once you develop the independence of your thumb and first and second fingers, you will notice a major change in your normal picking habits. This is because you will have strength-ened muscles that weren't used before.

Ex. 1

* T = thumb; 1 = index; 2 = middle

Ex. 2 has bass notes played with your thumb while your first and second fingers are playing the melody.

Ex. 2

In Ex. 3, I use the fingerpicking style on a rock/blues-type piece. Hopefully, these examples will help you to incorporate this style into your own vocabulary.

Ex. 3

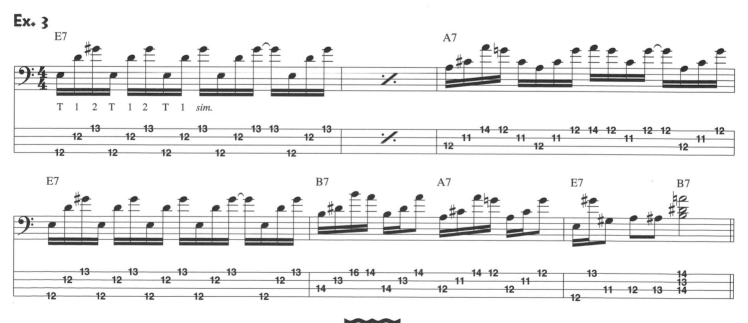

DIMINISHED SCALES

by Randy Coven
March 1989

The diminished scale is based on minor thirds (a step and a half or three frets). The diminished scale has nine notes and it is also known as a symmetrical scale, consisting of a half step followed by a whole step (Ex. 1A) or vice versa (Ex. 1B).

Ex. 1A G Symmetrical Diminished Scale (half step–whole step)

Ex. 1B G Symmetrical Diminished Scale (whole step–half step)

The diminished scale is similar to the whole tone scale, which also sounds like it has no discernible key center. Melodies and chords built on diminished scales are very different-sounding from those built on the diatonic harmony of the major scale we are used to hearing, and solos built on a diminished scale have a powerful and disorienting effect on the key center. See Ex. 2A and 2B. 2A is a diminished run using the 1, 3, 5, and 7 of the symmetrical diminished scale. Example 2B is a Randy Rhoads-type lick using a diminished run within an A harmonic minor scale.

Ex. 2A Diminished Run

Ex. 2B Diminished Run within a Harmonic Minor Scale

DIFFERENT RHYTHMS FOR CREATING BASS LINES

by Randy Coven
April 1989

Knowing about different types of rhythmic ideas, as found in musical styles such as country, soul, funk, rock, reggae and Brazilian, can be essential to your career as a bassist. Lead and melody instruments rely on a tight rhythm section in order to sound good. Ex. 1 is a country-style bass line. Notice the accents fall on beats one and three as opposed to the more conventional rock and funk examples, where the accents fall on two and four. To pick up on a modern country bass line, listen to "Pride O' the Farm," by the Dregs.

Ex. 1 Country

Ex. 2 is a funk and soul bass line similar to the new James Brown song "I'm Real."

Ex. 2 Soul/Funk

Ex. 3 features a typical heavy metal rock rhythm, where the eighth note is followed by two sixteenth notes. This is the staple for Steve Harris in Iron Maiden.

Ex. 3 Rock

Notice that in a reggae rhythm the bass line always starts on the upbeat of one. (Ex. 4.) Listen to any Bob Marley record to hear the finest in reggae bass lines.

There are two main types of rhythms used in Brazilian music, the Samba and the Bossa Nova. The Bossa Nova rhythm of Ex. 5 can be heard on the Steely Dan song "Rikki Don't Lose That Number."

The Samba is a faster version of the Bossa Nova and often uses more than just the standard root of fifth combination. See Ex. 6. For more with the Samba, listen to the appropriately named "Rio Samba," from the *Larry Carlton* album, also known as the 335 album.

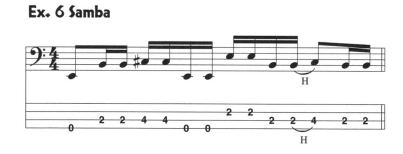

Play all these examples with a drummer or machine and experiment with your own ideas. While you're at it, listen to some of the finest rhythmic bass players, such as Anthony Jackson, Will Lee, Marcus Miller, Geddy Lee and Sting.

PENTATONIC SCALES

by Randy Coven
May 1989

Let's get familiar with the pentatonic sound. Whether or not you've recognized it as such, the pentatonic scale is one of the cornerstones of rock music and is also widely used in Japanese, Far Eastern, and African music. Pentatonic major and minor scales are both comprised of five notes, thus the name (Penta means five in Greek). Pentatonic major differs from a diatonic major scale in that two notes are left out, the 4th and the 7th. See Ex. 1.

Ex. 1 G Major   **G Pentatonic Major**

The pentatonic minor scale differs from the natural minor in that the 2nd and 6th notes are left out. See Ex. 2.

Ex. 2 G Natural Minor   **G Pentatonic Minor**

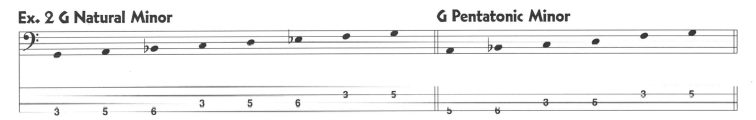

The pentatonic major scale sounds pretty familiar in the classic line from "Your Mama Don't Dance." See Ex. 3.

Ex. 3 à la "Your Mama Don't Dance"

The pentatonic minor may be familiar from the bridge in the James Gang classic, "Funk 49." See Ex. 4.

Ex. 4 à al "Funk 49"

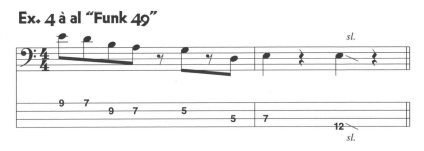

You've heard both of these scales countless times. Now try to use them yourself, recognize them in other music, and make them your own.

APPROACH NOTES

by Randy Coven
July 1989

There are four ways to "approach" a chord tone. The approach note is either a whole step or half step above or below. (Ex. 1.) This technique is most often used for creating walking bass lines for jazz changes, but it also can be used for funk lines, rock lines and making an ordinary walking blues line come alive.

Ex. 1

Half step below	Whole step below	Half step above	Whole step above

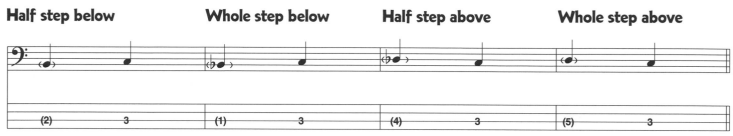

In Ex. 2 I've taken a blues funk riff that uses 1, 3, 5, 7 or the A7 chord, and approached each note from one half step below. You'll notice it has a Jaco-like sound.

Ex. 2

Ex. 3 is a walking blues line in A, using the approach note technique over the changes. It's like the bass line I used on "Full Tank," from the *Blues Saraceno* album. I use all the approach notes possible in this one. So to connect your chord changes and make them swing, it's as easy as using approach notes.

Ex. 3

*1/2A = half step above; 1A = whole step above; 1/2B = half step below; 1B = whole step below

SPEEDERCISES

by Randy Coven
September 1989

Being able to play fast is important these days. But part of being a good bassist is knowing what you can and cannot execute on the instrument. If you're playing a tune and go for a bass fill beyond your capabilities, you could sound like you're trying too hard as opposed to playing within your capabilities and sounding confident. Ex. 1 is designed for your right hand. It is a double stroking technique that I use to play fast triplets. You start on your second finger with a downstroke, followed by your first finger with a downstroke and an upstroke. Keep this picking pattern going until you feel you've got a type of circular motion with your right hand.

Ex. 1

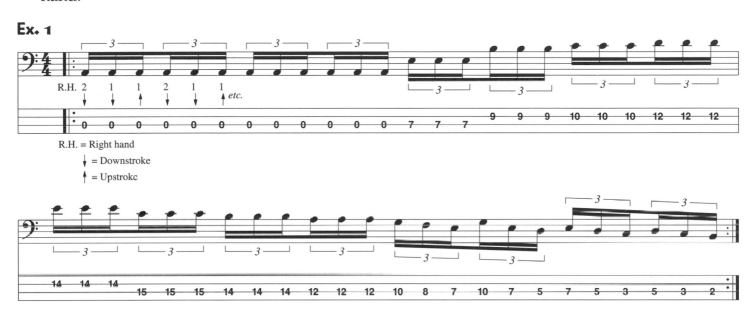

Ex. 2 is both hands, and can be used as a riff as well as an exercise. It is similar to a Vinnie Moore-type unison line you might hear him play with the bass on Mind's Eye. I also use this type of idea on the bridge to "Stuff It" from *Funk Me Tender*. Because it goes from the bottom of the neck to the top, you will be using the entire bass. Remember to start slowly and build up your speed. It's always better to do things perfectly at slower speeds than to sound sloppy by playing faster than your technique will allow.

Ex. 2

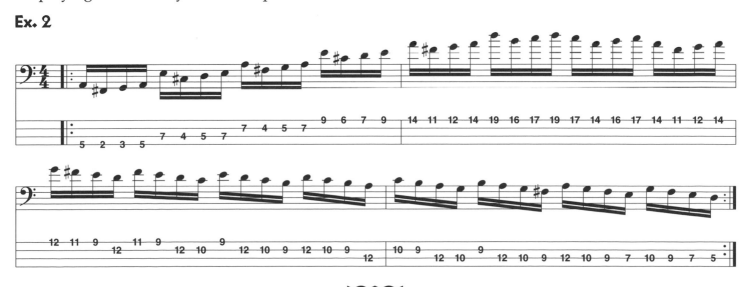

UP THE DOWN BASS NECK

by Randy Coven
October 1989

I've been getting a lot of requests to explain unison licks played between the bass and guitar. People often describe this lick as "the one going up and down the neck." A unison lick is the same lick played simultaneously between any two instruments. There are endless ways to approach writing these licks yourself. So let's look at how Steve Harris, Jaco Pastorius, Billy Sheehan and I approach this idea. Ex. 1 is a Steve Harris-type lick using 5ths.

Ex. 1 Steve Harris

Ex. 2 is what Jaco might do, taking a G major scale up the neck. His interval combinations with that scale would be mostly 4ths.

Ex. 2 Jaco Pastorius

Ex. 3 shows how Billy Sheehan might take a pattern of 3rds going up the neck, doubling the first note with fast triplets.

Ex. 3 Billy Sheehan

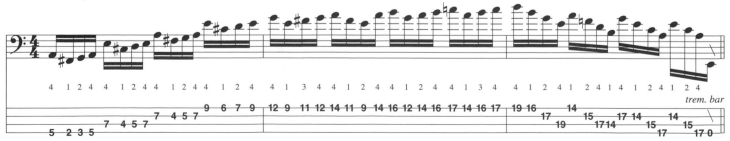

Ex. 4 is a bass secret of my own. Learn these licks, and then teach them to your guitar player and go up the down bass neck.

Ex. 4 Randy Coven

NATURAL TENSIONS

by Randy Coven
December 1989

If you've been reading this column regularly, you should know what an arpeggio is. Just in case you've forgotten, it's the notes of a chord, broken up and played one at a time. See Ex. 1 for a refresher.

Ex. 1

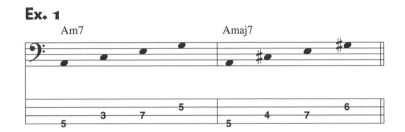

What we call natural tensions are the 9, 11 and 13 of any chord or scale. Ex. 2 is a two-octave A minor scale. I counted up to show you how easy it is to find the natural tensions.

Ex. 2 Tensions (9, 11, 13)

If I were to arpeggiate the A minor scale using the 1, 3, 5 and 7, I have the option of also adding the extended arpeggio 9, 11 and 13, thus creating an upper structure triad (Bm). See Ex. 3. Using this idea will add an extra dimension to your playing. If a guitar player is using an Am9 chord you might want to use the 9th instead of the more usual A root.

Ex. 3

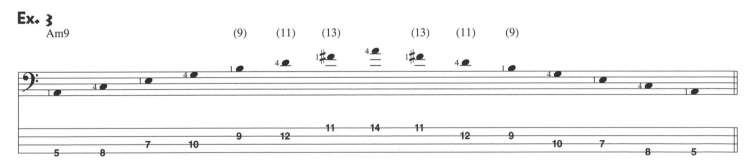

I use natural tensions a lot for soloing. Ex. 4 shows you a couple of ways to use natural tensions in the soloing context.

Ex. 4

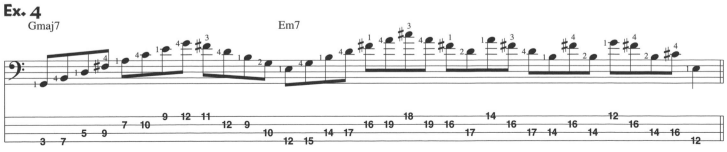

ALTERED TENSIONS

by Randy Coven
January 1990

This month we'll look at extended arpeggios with altered tensions. To review the natural tensions, I doubled the Mixolydian mode up to tensions 9, 11 and 13. See Ex. 1.

Ex. 1 E7 Mixolydian

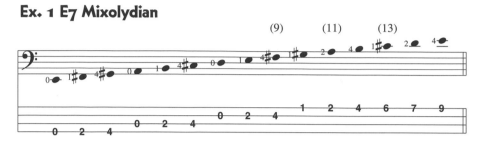

The altered tensions are created by altering the natural tensions. The altered tensions are flat 9, sharp 9, sharp 11 and flat 13. Altered tensions are used primarily with the Mixolydian mode. They're widely used in jazz and blues playing. If you play all the tensions together with the addition of the root, major 3 and flat 7, you will have played an altered scale. See Ex. 2.

Ex. 2 E Altered Scale

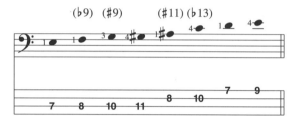

You can combine the Mixolydian mode with the altered scale (Ex. 1 and 2 together) and your solo and bass line possibilities will be endless. Ex. 3 will tie this all together. It's an E7 chord, using the arpeggios, tensions, the extensions of the altered tensions, and the altered scale, combined in different ways.

Ex. 3 E7 (Extended Arpeggios)

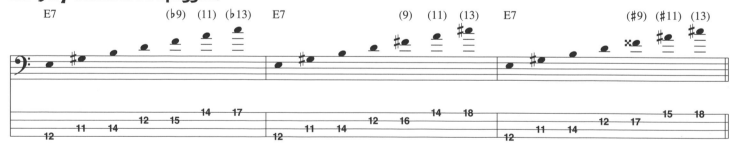

This sound might remind you of Vernon Reid, Jeff Berlin and Mike Stern.

Using Arpeggios in a Lick

TRICKS OF THE TRADE

by Randy Coven
February 1990

You hear them all the time, simple but effective licks that sound harder to play than they are. They are used mostly for fills and sometimes for bass lines. When you play these examples, you'll notice that they sound like you're doing a lot more than you are. Ex. 1 can be used as a bass line. It's an open-string triplet in Am. I got the idea from the Allman Brothers' "Whipping Post."

Ex. 1

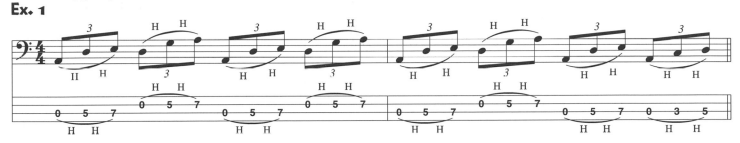

Ex. 2 is a variation of an open string ascending run, bouncing off random notes. This is a standard heavy metal trick. My concept is to hit notes that work harmonically with the open-string.

Ex. 2

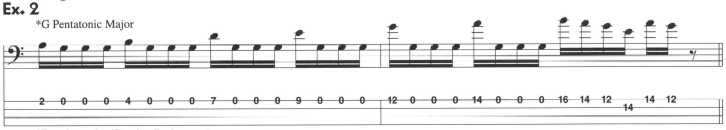

Ex. 3 sounds cool for a funk line or fill. It uses the hammer-on to sound like more notes than you're actually playing. I got the idea from listening to Jeff Berlin on "5G," from a Bill Bruford album.

Ex. 3

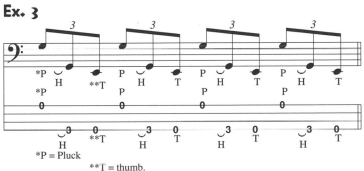

Ex. 4 is a simple trill. Instead of playing it straight, I've added a descending line with my picking hand. It shouldn't take long before you find these ideas easy to incorporate into your own playing.

Ex. 4

UP AND DOWN THE NECK

by Randy Coven
April 1990

I recently received a letter from a guy named Chris, who asked if Jaco Pastorius's bass part in "Birdland" had some tapping on it. The answer is no. To the best of my knowledge, Jaco never did any tapping. The only time his right hand went on the bass neck was to slide the palm of his hand down the E string, getting a percussive, conga-type soung. See Ex. 1 for a lick similar to what Jaco plays in "Birdland"; where there is a large skip up the neck to hit the doublestop, which is why Chris might have thought Jaco tapped it. It got me thinking of some exercises which will help make it less scary to jump around on the bass neck.

Ex. 1

Ex. 2 is something I learned from Steve Vai. It's hitting the same note in octaves all over the neck.

Ex. 2

Ex. 3 is a smooth way to jump around the neck. You hit an open string between the skip, making the open string a part of the lick.

Ex. 3

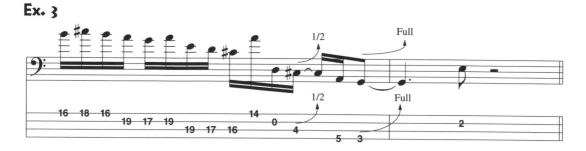

Ex. 4 is one string arpeggios, both major and minor.

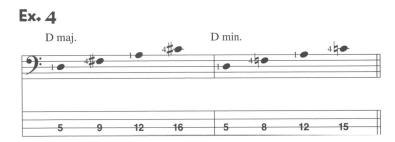

Ex. 5 involved practicing the same riff in two different octaves, jumping back and forth.

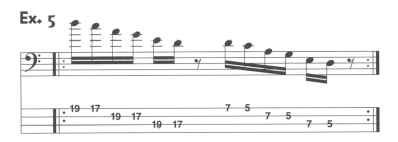

TAPPING INTO THE MODES

by Randy Coven
August 1990

I believe learning the modes is the single most important musical thing you can do to improve your playing ability. This process can be very tedious, but the end result is well worth it. In this column, I will show you some tapping licks that I came up with to make learning the modes easier and more fun.

I'll also show you a quick way to recognize what key you're in when playing in any given mode. There's no point in playing in a modal position without knowing what key it's related to. Without this understanding, you can be stuck in the same old box position, only this time it will be a mode. That defeats the whole purpose of learning the modes, which is to open up the neck. For a look at the modes, see Ex. 1.

Ex. 1 Modes in G Major

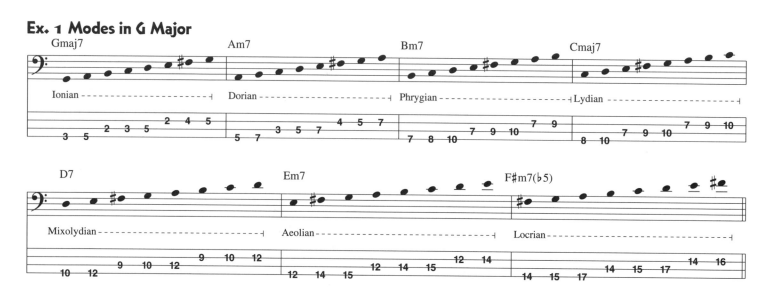

Ex. 2 is a tapping exercise which taps out the root, 5th, octave and 3rd of each mode. While playing this, say the names of the modes to yourself as you do them in order.

Ex. 2 Tapping

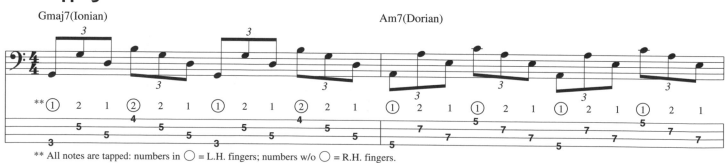

** All notes are tapped: numbers in ◯ = L.H. fingers; numbers w/o ◯ = R.H. fingers.

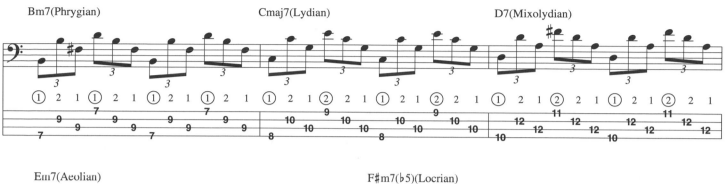

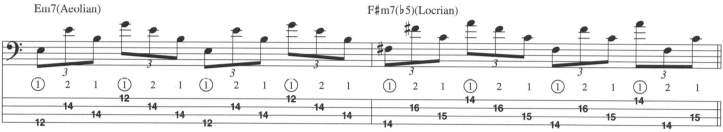

Knowing the order of the modes will lead you naturally to the next segment of the column—finding the key they relate to. Ex. 3 shows you how to do this. Observe the order of the modes and simply count back the degree of whatever mode you're in. For example: E Dorian is the second degree of something. What you do is go up the E Dorian scale and count back two from the octave. Always start your count with the octave as one. Whatever note you land on is the key you're in—in this case D.

Ex. 3 should make this very clear. Stay with this lesson a while now and come back to it from time to time if you need a brush up.

Ex. 3 Finding the Key You're In

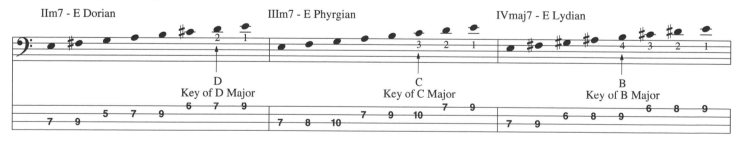

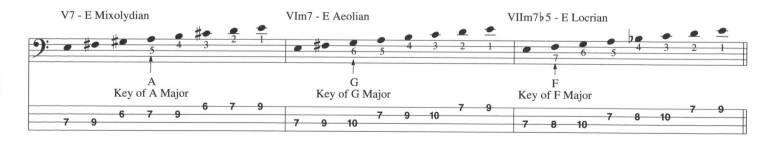

BREATHE IN THE AIR

by Stu Hamm
September 1992

Let's start off with the most basic instinct that there is—breathing! I'm assuming that since most of you reading this are alive, you already know the basic ins and outs of breathing, but how many of you remember to do so while you are playing?

It is extremely important to be loose and relaxed while you are playing, and breathing deeply and evenly is one of the best ways to ease tension of any kind. Hindus and Buddhists have written volumes on the art of meditation, so if any of you are especially moved by this article, there is much literature at your disposal.

There are many ways and reasons to tense up while you are playing, and they are all a great impediment to your playing. Say that you are playing a song that has a very difficult passage in the bridge, a fast run or something. Even while you're playing the rest of the song, you're thinking, "Oh no, that hard part is coming up. Sure hope I get it right!" While you're thinking this, the muscles in your arms, wrists and fingers tense up, until you have a vise-like grip on your bass, making it impossible to play anything!

I'm sure you all know people who stop breathing when they are soloing. I used to have this problem. I'd get so worked up that I'd turn bright red in the face and my breath would come out in short, labored spurts. My muscles tensed up, and I'm sure it sounded that way in the music, so here are some exercises that I came up with that helped me, and that will hopefully help you, as well.

I wrote a piece called "Simple Dreams" for my first album, *Radio Free Albemuth.* The chordal bass part I wrote as a sort of meditation exercise. It's a slow, melancholy piece and what I do is breathe in deeply through the nose during the first bar, then, when the chord changes during the second bar, breathe out slowly and deeply through my mouth. Then you try to play the piece feeling the rhythm of your breathing. This is a very, very simple exercise that I do as a regular part of my warm-up exercises, and it's amazing how much a few minutes of deep breathing will relax your body and focus your mind.

Play a G major scale, slowly, and while going up the scale, breathe in slowly and deeply through the nose. When you get to the top G, stop for a moment, then as you play the scale back down, breathe out through your mouth. Breathe in the good air, and exhale the bad air! You can take any piece you play, divide it into groups of bars, and arrange a breathing pattern around it. I'm not saying that you need to inhale and exhale in time with the music while performing, but if you take the time to practice this, it will become second nature, and you will find yourself much more at ease in any situation.

So, until next time, relax, take a deep breath, let it out, feel the wonderful rhythm of your breathing and let 'er rip! Ta-Ta!

TWO-OCTAVE SCALES

by Stu Hamm
October, 1992

One thing I've noticed that a lot of young or beginning players have trouble with is moving up and down the neck in a fluid manner (i.e, changing hand positions, etc.). I'm going to give you some tips on how to make these transitions smoother and more musical.

With any scale or line, there are many different ways to finger it, and many different positions on the neck to play it in. For example, the same note as the open G string can be played on the fifth fret of the D string, the 10th fret of the A string, and the 15th fret of the E string. Where you play this note will depend on the notes that precede it, and where the line goes after it. Keep in mind that the tone or sound of the G is very different in the four spots where it can be played. This sound also factors into your decision as to which one to use.

For example, in Ex. 1, the G Major scale starts way up on the neck, the 15th fret of the E. Now, check out Ex. 2, which starts on the 10th fret of the A string. It should sound a little smoother than Ex. 1.

Note that both of these fingerings cross three strings. Since each string has its own timbre, using three different strings can make it sound a little unsmooth. Ex. 3, which starts on the 5th fret of the D string, uses only two strings and incorporates slides.

Ex. 1

Ex. 2

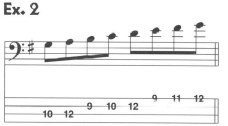

Ex. 3

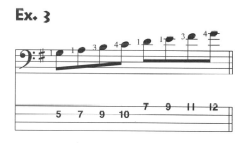

See what a more even sound it has when played like this! The point I'm trying to make is that when moving up and down the neck you should… well… MOVE UP AND DOWN the neck, not straight across it.

Now practice Ex. 4, which is a two-octave G Major scale. When you slide, be sure your fingers are already in position to play the next notes.

Ex. 4

Try to incorporate this technique in everything you play, and you'll achieve a smoother and more fluid tone! Keep rockin'!

USING OPEN STRINGS

by Stu Hamm
November 1992

There are pluses and minuses to using open strings. In general, I try to avoid them as much as possible, except when trying to achieve a certain effect. Just as we saw last month, that by playing the same note in different positions you get different sounds, playing an open note will usually sound brighter and have more sustain. For example: Playing a G Major scale using open strings will sound a little disjointed (See Ex. 1). The proper way to finger this scale is shown in Ex. 2. Notice how much smoother it is!

There are times, though, that you can use an open string to your advantage, especially when trying to move up and down the neck quickly.

I first came upon this technique when trying to figure out the fingerings for a series of quick arpeggios in a piece by Claude Debussy entitled "Dr. Gradus Ad Patnasum" for my first solo album, *Radio Free Albumuth*. I found that it was possible to use an open string to jump between two hand positions instead of sliding and using three or four hand positions! This is how it works: (See Ex. 3).

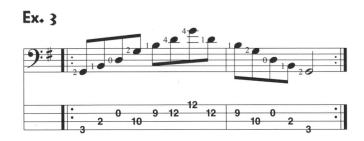

It is important that when you are playing the open D, immediately move your left hand into the next position; with your middle finger on the G on the D string and your fourth finger on the G, 12th fret of the G string; then your first finger should be in place for the B, and the fourth for the D. Here's another example, combining a G Major and C Major arpeggio.

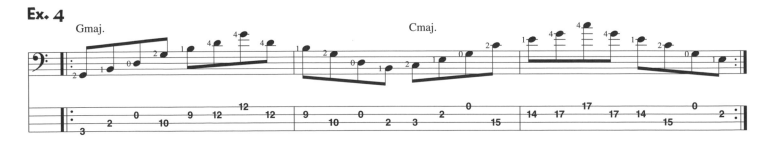

The lesson to be learned: open strings—use them, but don't abuse them!!

HOW TO BECOME A BETTER BASS PLAYER

by Stu Hamm
December 1992

Hello, readers! This month I thought I would pass on some tips I've learned that will help you become a better bassist and a better musician.

Practice, Practice, Practice!

There will come a time when you will have to do some serious shedding (locking yourself in a woodshed and practicing 24 hours a day). Musicians in general seem to have a rap for not being particularly disciplined. If you suffer from this problem, I suggest you make a checklist and stick to it daily: maybe one hour sight reading, one hour improvisation, one hour slapping practice, etc. If you are a beginner and do not read music, get yourself a beginner's book and learn to do so.

Here is a way that I often practice. Take something extremely difficult, something you think you can never play. Figure it out *slowly*—don't be in a rush to play it fast. Set your metronome or click-track at a slow speed and play it every day. Then increase the speed of the metronome slowly every day. If you can get beyond the frustration, you can only play it better every day!

When I first got the idea to play "Linus & Lucy" it took me forever to work it out, and I thought that when I had it I really would have accomplished something. But the great thing is that when I could play it, I realized that I had only seen the tip of the iceberg, and that that piece was a launching pad for a whole new set of goals and techniques.

If you ever feel that you've "done it" and don't need to practice any more, I suggest you take up something else.

Go Fly a Kite

Even though discipline is a must, there *is* such a thing as beating a dead horse. You will know when you are just going through the motions and not getting anywhere. Read a book, see a movie, go play golf, take a walk in the woods. Experience life!!! Then you can come back and approach your bass in a fresh, new way. Try to incorporate your day-to-day feelings, hurts, loves, and needs into your playing. This is the key to being an artist—a musician—and not merely a technician.

Listen to Other Bass Players

A lot of my early years consisted of taking bass lines from records. I figured out how to play "The Real Me," one of the great bass lines of all time, by John Entwistle of The Who off of *Quadrophenia.* Then it was Chris Squire of Yes—I got kicked out of a practice room in high school for playing the live version of "The Fish" at extreme volume. Then, for me, it was

Stanley Clarke. And when I first saw Jaco Pastorius play, I immediately ripped the frets out of my bass and put my hair in corn rows!

Every new generation is an outgrowth of what came before. Even the great innovators like Charles Mingus, Jaco, and Bill Sheehan (although they were quantum leaps) followed an orderly progression out of what preceded them.

So don't be afraid to work out licks from Flea, Jason Newsted, Les Claypool, Billy, myself or whomever. This is called "learning the alphabet."

Don't Listen to Anyone

After you have learned the alphabet, you will reach a point when you will start to want to make up your own words, then a sentence, then a paragraph. Your career goal is to write your own book. You certainly will be influenced by others and maybe, for a time, sound a lot like your favorite player. But every one of you reading this has something special—something unique that no one else has or can duplicate. When you find this, go the distance, follow this path as far as you can. Sing the song *in your own voice* and write your novel. Do this, and you are bound to be successful!!! Good Luck!

A FEW NOTES ON SOLOING

by Stu Hamm
January 1993

This month, I thought that I would pass along some ideas that hopefully will help your soloing. That's right, every now and then your guitar player will get tired of hearing himself play and pass the baton to you. This won't occur very often so you have to be ready!

Soloing is much more than how many notes you can play. Every so often the bassist actually gets to solo over the changes of a song, or gets to take a few choruses over a blues. This is the most challenging form because it requires the bassist to be musical, so here are some things to think about when you are faced with this challenge.

Quoting the Melody

This is a standard part of soloing you should be familiar with. "Quoting" means restating or interpreting the original melody. You can transpose it to another key, change the phrasing of it, or bass-icly do anything to it so that the listener will be reminded of (or will recognize) the melody, without your actually playing it note for note. This will give your solo, and the entire song, more continuity.

Rhythmic Phrasing

This consists of taking a certain rhythm and using it with a variety of notes. It can be of any length but the idea is that by repeating this phrase, you will build tension and excitement. A well thought-out solo uses tension and release to get its point across. Listen to Yes's "Close To The Edge" suite which is built entirely on tension and release.

Soloing

Your solo should be about feeling and moods, not merely notes. So here is an exercise that I often use to get that point across when teaching. Practice soloing over a standard blues form and see how many different moods you can create. Try to play a chorus that sounds happy. Make one sound sad. Play one that sounds angry and one that sounds like you are in love. This sounds a lot easier than it is! Try this out on other people and see if they can guess what emotion you are trying to express. Don't be afraid to over-exaggerate—it's a great way to learn.

Now for the killer. Using the same idea, play choruses using only one note. Neil Young is famous for this. That's right, you can play a whole chorus with just one note and make it sound happy, sad, angry, lovely, frustrated, etc.

The great thing about this particular exercise is that it forces you to use things like dynamics and phrasing that often get lost in a furry of notes. You may think this exercise sounds silly, but try it and you will see how difficult it actually is.

CHORDS FOR THE BASSIST, PART 1

by Stu Hamm
February 1993

One of the ways that bass playing has changed over the years is that today many more bass players are using chords, either for soloing or for accompaniment purposes. One of the first chordal bass solos that I ever heard was in the song "Bouree" by Jethro Tull, a truly inspired solo, well ahead of its time. I urge you all to check it out if you haven't heard it before. Another early influence on my playing was Chris Squire's live version of "The Fish" on *Yessongs*. Both of these solos were very "guitar oriented"; that is, using a pick and strumming chords. Jeff Berlin was one of the first to use chords in more of a jazz vein (i.e., using more complex chord voicings and plucking with his fingers). With the popularization of tapping techniques, there is a slew of great new bassists continually pushing the envelope further. Check out the intricacy and beauty of Victor Wooten's playing with Bela Fleck & The Flecktones and the off-the-wall ostinatos of Primus' Les Claypool. OUTSTANDING.

Playing chords has become such an integral part of being a modern bassist that it is essential to be familiar with its basics and applications.

This month we'll be talking about basic triads. A triad is a chord made up of three notes. A basic triad contains the root, third, and fifth notes of the scale. It is the third that determines whether a chord is major or minor. A major third is two whole steps above the root. So, a C major triad would be C, E, and G. A minor third is one whole step and one half step above the root. So, a C minor triad would be C, Eb, and G. Ex. 1 shows how these are played. Let your hands get used to these positions, so that you can instinctively form a major or minor triad.

Ex. 1

C Major   C Minor

Ex. 2 shows a different voicing of the same triads, but with the root and fifth anchoring the bottom, and with the third on top.

Ex. 2

C Major   C Minor

Seventh chords are made by adding (obviously) the seventh note of the scale. We'll be talking about three different kinds of seventh chords today: the major 7th, dominant 7th and minor 7th, the three most common 7th chords you will encounter. Here is how they are formed:

Major 7th: This is formed with the root, major third, fifth, and major seventh. In the key of C that's C, E, G, B.

Dominant 7th: This is formed with the root, major third, fifth, and flatted (or "dominant") seventh. In the key of C that's C, E, G, B♭. The dominant 7th is the predominant chord used in the blues.

Minor 7th: This is formed with the root, minor third, fifth, and flatted seventh. In the key of C: C, E♭, G, B♭.

"But wait," I hear you cry. "If you are to play a three-note chord and the chord has four notes, what do we do?" Not to worry. The common bond between the chords is the root and fifth. Obviously, you have to play the root to establish tonality. The fifth is so strong that it is almost taken for granted—the ear will hear it even if it isn't played. It is the third or seventh that gives the chord its flavor. So, a 7th chord triad will consist of the root, third, and seventh.

Exs. 3–5 show the different ways to play the 7th triads, first by playing root, third, seventh, and then root, seventh, third.

Once again, get the fingerings memorized. And try playing them at different positions around the neck. Some voicings will sound better on different parts of the neck. For beginners, I suggest trying to figure out the different 7th chords in all keys.

This article should give you the basic theory behind building a chord when you are just given a chord symbol, and also a beginning feel for the patterns of these chords.

Good luck!

CHORDS FOR THE BASSIST, PART 2

by Stu Hamm
Guitar, March, 1993

Greetings, fellow bassists!

This month I'd like to introduce you to some of the more common four-note chords. We'll learn 7th chords, 9th chords, 6th chords, sus4 chords, and then there will be a piece that you can play which I have written using these chords to familiarize you with their sounds and fingerings.

An Em7 chord will consist of the root, minor 3rd, 5th, and minor 7th (Ex.1).

Note that when playing this chord, you form a bar across all four strings with your first finger. To change that chord to an E dominant 7th chord (E7), your second finger frets the G♯, making the chord major (Ex. 2).

Playing an Emaj7 chord is a bit tricky, so here are two alternate fingerings (Exs. 3 & 4). I know these feel awkward, but I promise that they won't permanently ruin your hands.

A 7sus4 chord is when you suspend the resolution by playing a 4th and then resolving it to the 3rd (Exs. 5 and 6). Stanley Clarke has used this to great effect.

When we are playing a 6th chord, we add a 6th to a triad, so a 6th chord would consist of the root, 3rd, 5th and 6th. Here is the Em♭6, remembering that we use a flatted 6th and a minor 3rd (Ex. 7). Another pretty tough one to finger, but a beautiful chord. To make it a major 6th we simply move the minor 3rd and flatted 6th to major 3rd and major 6th (Ex. 8).

The minor add9 chord is again a very haunting chord with the minor 9th (same note as the minor 2nd, one octave up) creating tension next to the minor 3rd (Ex. 9). In Ex. 10 we have an Eadd9 chord.

There you have it! A list and explanation of some of the most typical chords that I use when playing chords. I am sure that you will hear many parts of many familiar tunes as you work with these chords (the bridge to Satriani's "Always With Me, Always With You" for one) and that you will be able to create beautiful music of your own with them.

"A New Day" is a piece I've written using these chords. Pay special attention to the fingering and enjoy yourselves!

"A New Day"

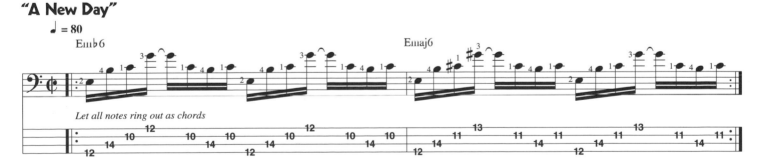

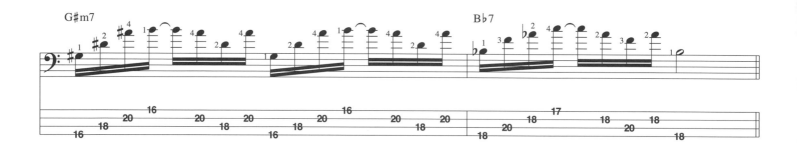

Keep practicing.

NATURAL HARMONICS

by Stu Hamm
April 1993

Harmonics are the natural series of overtones on your strings that appear in a very ordered, mathematical sequence—that explains why they appear where they do. Not being a mathematician, I will not go into this aspect, as there are many good books which deal with that. What I intend to do in these articles is expose you to the basics and some applications. Hopefully this will inspire you to search out new uses of them in your playing and writing.

To get started, let's play a G on the twelfth fret of your G string. To play the harmonic, simply lift your finger up so it is still on the string but not pushing it down to the fretboard. Now play the note and move your finger off the string to let it vibrate freely. You will hear the same note with a little different sound. See, folks, it's just that simple! Notice that this is exactly halfway between the bridge and the nut. Now, if you go halfway between the twelfth fret and the nut in actual distance, not number of frets, you will be on the fifth fret. Play this harmonic and you will hear a G one octave higher. This works the same way between the twelfth fret and the bridge, so if you play the harmonic where the 24th fret would be you will get the same note. Naturally, this works the same way on all four strings.

Now play the harmonic on the seventh fret and you will hear the fifth (or D on the G string) an octave higher than the fretted D. Now, play the twelfth fret harmonics from low E to high G, and then the seventh fret harmonics the same way and you will see where the great Chris Squire got the inspiration for his bass feature "The Fish."

Now, the higher the harmonics go, the less they line up with the frets. All the ones we have talked about so far should be played right over the fret. To get our next one, you have to play just behind the fourth fret, and you will get a major third, or B♮ on the G string.

Now play the harmonic just after the third fret and you will get another fifth (or D on the G string). If you keep moving your finger slowly towards the nut you will get a slightly out of tune dominant seventh and another octave. These are pretty hard to get, so we'll deal with the others first. Here is the scale you can play using harmonics on the third, fourth, and fifth frets: First, play Ex. 1 actually fretting the notes. Sounds like something from a *Johnny Quest* soundtrack, doesn't it? Now play the same fingering, but this time playing the harmonics. Sounds quite different, doesn't it? Here is the scale that the harmonics make it, although it is actually a couple of octaves higher (Ex. 2).

There you have the A–B–C's of harmonics. Hopefully you will practice enough to learn the whole alphabet and then start making up your own words. See ya!!

Ex. 1

Ex. 2

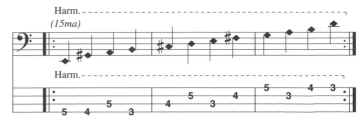

ARTIFICIAL HARMONICS

~~~

by Stu Hamm
May 1993

In addition to natural harmonics; that is, the harmonics that are available on the open strings, there are, natural other ways to create harmonics, and these are called "artificial harmonics." In this month's column I am going to discuss several of the ways they can be created.

We learned that halfway between the nut and the bridge is the spot where you will get the harmonic and octave above the note that would be fretted there. The same theory applies not only to the nut but also with a note that you fret with your left hand. For example, if you fret the C on the fifth fret on the G string, the halfway point between that and the bridge would be the C an octave higher, or on the 17th fret. Now the question is, with one hand tied up fretting the note, how do you get the harmonic to ring out? Well, there are a couple of ways that you can accomplish this.

The first way is to tap it, or drum your fingers. John Entwistle is famous for drumming his fingers across the strings. It's the same technique as tapping or drumming your fingers on the table in irritation while you wait for your date to get dressed so you can get to the show in time. This is how John played those great bass breaks in The Who's "My Generation." Also, depending on where you tap on the fretboard you will get a lot of interesting overtones.

So, while fretting the C on the fifth fret of the G string, tap the C right on the fret of the 17th fret. It is important to hit it firmly, and to release your finger quickly so that the note can ring out. This is how I played one half of the bass duet in the song "Surely the Best" on my *Kings of Sleep* CD.

This works across the whole neck, simply tapping the fret one octave above the one that you are fretting with your left hand. This technique does not work well though if you want to produce an artificial harmonic in which you are fretting a note above the 12th fret. For this we will use another technique, the "Jaco Pinch." This technique is what the great Jaco Pastorius made famous in the intro to "Birdland" off the album *Heavy Weather* by Weather Report. This technique involves stopping the string and plucking it at the same time.

There are two ways to do it. Once again fretting the C on the fifth fret of the G string, put the thumb of your right hand over the C on the 17th fret, not pushing it down but merely resting on the string with your thumb pointing towards the ground and your hand across the strings. Now, with your first finger pull up on the string and pluck it, again making sure to remove your thumb after the initial attack to allow the string to ring.

If you are fretting a note above the 12th fret, like Jaco when he frets the 14th in "Birdland," you might have to search around for the exact spot, since most basses don't have more than 24 frets, but you'll eventually find that spot that is halfway to the bridge.

The other way to achieve this is to use your first finger to stop the note and use your second or third finger to pluck it. I find this a little clumsier, but many players use it. Also, while playing it this way, you will look like Chico Marx when he would "shoot" notes on the piano.

Artificial harmonics, virtual reality, what's next?

~~~

SLIDING HARMONICS

by Stu Hamm
June 1993

This month I'd like to offer a few more words on harmonics and show you a piece of mine that uses many of the harmonic techniques we've been discussing.

We've talked about true harmonics and artificial harmonics. Now I'd like to introduce you to another way you can use them—that is sliding harmonics. Although I'm sure that the fundamentals of this technique are rooted in antiquity, the first people I became aware of who use this style are two bass players: Percy Jones (of the band Brand X) and Bunny Brunel. To hear this technique used to its fullest, I strongly suggest that you check out some of their albums. Jeff Ament uses it in Pearl Jam's "Evenflow." These players primarily use this technique on fretless basses. Though it is much easier to get a good tone and sustain this way, it's possible with practice to achieve the same effect on a fretted bass so let's get started.

Hit your open harmonic on the 12th fret of your G string, then push your fingers down on the fret and slide it up to the 14th fret. See how that works? Now play the 12th fret G harmonic and slide it down to the 9th fret to get an E. Now, hit your harmonic on the 5th fret of the G string and slide it to the 7th fret. This gives the same notes as the first example but an octave higher. This may take some practice but you will get it.

Sliding harmonics enables you to create chords that you can't get using just regular harmonics. Here are two examples:

For a C triad, hit the open harmonic on the 12th fret on the G string, then play the harmonic on the 12th fret of the D string and slide it up to the 14th fret, giving you and E, and then finger the C on the 15th fret of the A string (Ex. 1). Make sure to let all the notes ring out.

Ex. 1

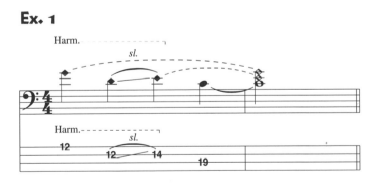

For a D chord, play the 7th fret harmonics on the G and D strings. Then play the 7th fret harmonic on the A string, slide it up to the 9th fret and then finger the D on the 10th fret of the E string (Ex. 2). With a little experimentation you'll be able to come up with lots of interesting chords.

Ex. 2

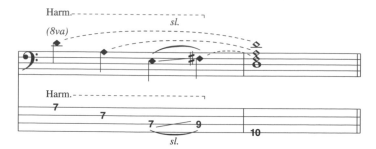

Finally, here is a transcription of the bass intro to my song "Surely the Best" off my *Kings of Sleep* album (Ex. 3).

The upper part uses the tapping method of artificial harmonics. The TAB will show you where to finger the notes with your left hand, and with your right hand you will be tapping the fret an octave higher. The lower part uses open harmonics with a couple of slides. Try playing this with another bass player or on tape to get it to sound like it does on the record. And remember, Pete Rose always slid in head first!

Ex. 3 "Surely the Best" (Intro)

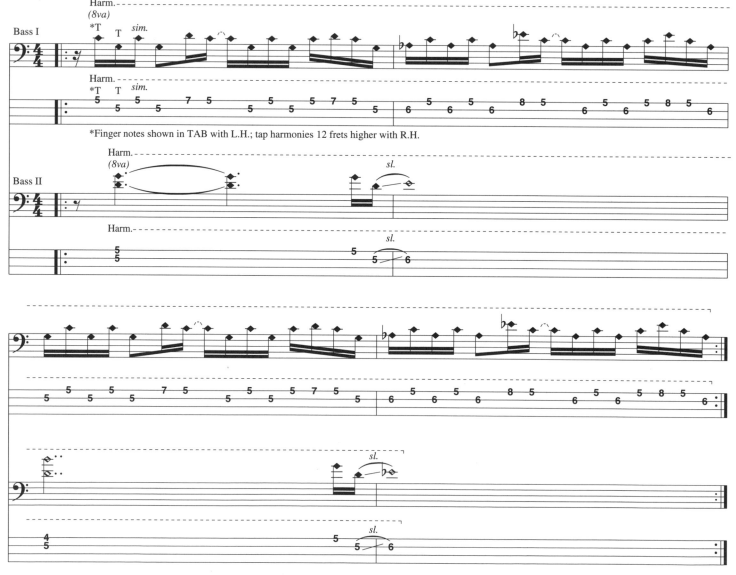

*Finger notes shown in TAB with L.H.; tap harmonies 12 frets higher with R.H.

THREE ON THREE

by Stu Hamm
July, 1993

Hello again, readers. No, this article is not on a hockey game with way too many penalties —sorry, inside sports joke for my friends north of the border—but rather I'd like to show you a couple of ways of popping the triplet figure. This figure is prominent in all forms of music and when mastered can be a useful tool, as a quick fill together with your drummer, for example.

Ex. 1 is the basis from which we will work. We are going to use the same rhythmic pattern while we discuss three different basic techniques to play the same figure.

Ex. 1 is a simple snap of the wrist to get you loosened up. If you tense up your wrist while popping and slapping, you're not only going to develop wrist problems, but it just won't sound smooth. So it's all in the wrist, which you should keep as loose and relaxed as possible. This is especially important when you play the last E of the triplet figure and the final half note E after it. Instead of actually moving your wrist and re-attacking both or these notes, if your wrist is nice and loose you actually just bounce your thumb against the string (sort of like the way a drummer would play a press roll).

Ex. 1

*T = thumb (slap); P = pop.

Ex. 2 is an extension of the same idea. All of the triplets figure will be played by bouncing your thumb on the E. First, try it with your wrist tight, re-attacking each note, then loosen it up and practice the bouncing technique. This will take some practice but as you become more adept at the bounce, I'm sure you will see how much better and easier and cleaner it is to play it this way.

Ex. 2

Ex. 3 is a different permutation, using the same "bouncing thumb" technique.

Ex. 3

Ex. 4 uses what I call a "dead note slap" with the left hand. The second note of the triplet (designated by x) is more of a sound than an actual note. Start off by playing it as a hammer-on to the 9th fret. Then use your second, third and fourth fingers to slap against the neck, making a clicking sound. To practice this, anchor your first finger on the fretboard and then slap with the remaining fingers, using the bottom of your knuckles to get a sound while slapping the strings. Remember, we are going for a click or sound, and not an actual note. This is a technique that I use quite a bit and when mastered can be played very quickly, but remember to always practice it slowly at first to achieve proper technique.

Ex. 4

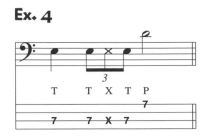

Ex. 5 is a "Flamenco Rake" technique that uses your first and second fingers to pop individual notes. So, set yourself up with your thumb on the A string, your first finger under the D string and your middle finger under the G string. What we don't do is pull up with the first and second fingers, but what we do is keep them totally rigid. Then, after you slap the E twice, pull your wrist away from the bass in a flicking motion, thumb over the top towards the G string. As your wrist moves, your first and second fingers will come up and pop the D and G strings, but remember to keep your fingers stiff. This is a hard one to master but with patience and practice anything can be accomplished. These techniques are covered in my instructional video *Slap Pop & Tap* on Hot Licks Videos as well as more advanced popping on my second video due out this summer. If there are other slapping techniques you have seen or heard me play, please write and I will try to discuss them in future articles.

Ex. 5

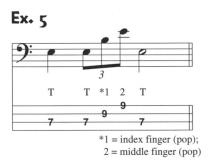

*1 = index finger (pop);
2 = middle finger (pop)

Ex. 6 is based on the main groove from a song entitled "Count Zero" from my *Kings of Sleep* CD. It uses the "raking" technique, and after popping the E with your middle finger, bring your thumb back down to slap the same note and then pop the B on the G string. Remember to roll the wrist and this should give you hours of fun (or frustration) trying to get it.

Ex. 6

So until the next time, practice, patience, practice, patience....

LEARN THESE SONGS... FAST

by Stu Hamm
Guitar, August 1993

How many times has this happened to you? A bass playing friend of yours get sick, or you get recommended for a gig, and someone gives you a tape and says, "Learn these 20 songs by tomorrow." Well, it's happened to me on many occasions, so this month I thought that I would pass along some tips and shortcuts to learning a song and some shorthand for writing out a chart.

The first thing to do, obviously, is listen to the song over and over, or "live" with it for a while. Get a feel for the mood and feel of the piece. Make a note of trouble spots (i.e., licks, modulations, tricky rhythms) so that when you are writing your road map you will know where the hazard signs are.

The next step is to map out the form of the songs. When you've played as many different songs as I have, from Elvis tunes and Top 40 covers to Satriani's songs, you will find that there is a common form to most pop tunes. They can usually be divided into Intro, Verse, Chorus, Bridge (or solo section) and Vamp. So as you next listen to the song, write out the form as it goes by, like Intro 8 bars, V_1 (Verse 1) 16 bars, Chorus 8 bars, V_2 (Verse 2) 16 bars, 2x Chorus (double chorus) 16 bars, Bridge 16 bars, V_3 (Verse 3) 16 bars, Chorus vamp out. All of this should be done before you even pick up your bass. Then, on regular paper, you can write an abbreviated form chart. For instance, I would write the previous song like this:

| I 8 | V_1 16 | C 8 | V_2 16 ‖: | C 8 :‖ | B 16 | V_3 16 ‖: | C 8 :‖ |

Note how I use the repeat signs. When trying to memorize a song, nothing helps more than to write it down while you are working on it. Once you have the form it's simply a matter of filling in the blanks!

Now you pick up your bass and start to learn the chords and rhythms. At this point you should call up whomever gave you the tape and make sure that you know what key the song is in. You can usually hear the open E's and A's—that will give you a clue. But if it's a tape that has been copied and re-copied on a tape deck with different speeds, a song in the key of C can easily sound like B or C#.

If the song has a recurring riff, then get out your music paper and write it down. Again, this will help in memorization and whenever this appears in the song, you can notate it by writing "lick" or "riff."

Now figure out the basic chords of the verse and chorus and write them out. Then make a map of the rhythms: say a song has a syncopated verse and a chorus of straight eighth notes—write down the pattern of the syncopation. The general shorthand for straight eighths is ♪ or you could write it as ♫ .

Now by filling in the holes you should be able to make a workable chart for the song. SOME NOTES: ideally you will have time to write out a complete chart on music paper. But if you develop a shorthand technique of your own, something like I've shown you here, you can save yourself some time (and trees), especially on the easier songs.

If you get to a particular fast or complicated line, try to get the basic shape and rhythm of it instead of trying to kill yourself going over and over the same half bar. Your tape heads do not like this. If you can approximate it and know its shape, it's very easy to have the guitar or keys (whoever is doubling the line) physically show you the line or notes in rehearsal, since I've noticed that a lot of "fast licks" are just fingering patterns played at various points of the neck. So don't panic!

Lastly, try to find spaces where you can be yourself and put a bit of your own personality into the music. This is a judgment call that only you can make. Obviously if it's a band doing Top 40 or cover tunes then you want to play it pretty straight. But if it's an original band, you'll sense places where your own personality can come into play. For instance, when the song is vamping out and the bass player plays some fills, put your own in, unless it is an ensemble part where the whole band plays certain accents. People are generally looking for a musician, not a machine. Here's a good example:

When I auditioned guitar players for the *Urge* tour for my last album, I asked them to learn the song "Long Star," which featured a brilliant solo by Eric Johnson. I couldn't believe my ears when guitar player after guitar player came in and played Eric's solo note for note! At that point in the song I wanted to hear what each guy would do with it, what he could add to my band. But finally, my fellow *Guitar* columnist Alex Skolnick came in and took the song to a place I'd never heard it before! So he was the man! Moral of my story: work hard and be original!!

Well, story time's over… back to work!!!

~~~

TWO-HAND TAPPING

by Stu Hamm
September 1993

Since I really haven't covered much about tapping in these articles, I thought that this month would be a good one for touching on some of the basic skills. So here's your crash course on contrapuntal tapping!

First of all, when tapping you must pay close attention to hand position. Your fingers must be well-curved so that you are pushing the strings down at a perfect right angle. If you don't, you will push the string out of tune and you won't get as much ring and sustain out of the string.

If you are just starting to tap I suggest that you start by practicing the right and left hands separately at first and then put the two together. There is nothing really difficult about the fingering or examples, but what we are aiming for is coordination and independence of the two hands.

Ex. 1 has the root and fifth of G in the left hand while the right runs the first part of a G major scale. This is the easiest of all the exercises because your right and left hands are playing the exact same rhythms, so it shouldn't give you too many problems.

Ex. 1

* *8va* refers to upstemmed notes only (for all examples).
** All upstemmed notes are R.H. taps; all downstemmed notes are L.H. taps (for all examples).

In Ex. 2 we double up the right hand to quarters while keeping the left in half notes.

Ex. 2

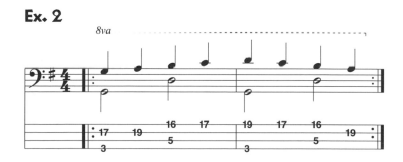

Ex. 3 swaps that around—quarters with the left and half notes with the right. If you have trouble at first, try to play the half notes without thinking about them and concentrate on the quarters.

Ex. 3

In Ex. 4 things start to heat up a little with the syncopated rhythm in the left hand.

Ex. 4

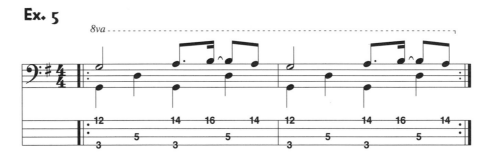

Ex. 5 has the syncopation in the right hand, and the left hand straight. These two exercises should start to develop independence of the two hands.

Ex. 5

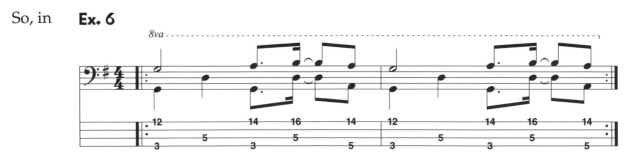

Ex. 6 uses the syncopation in both hands.

So, in **Ex. 6**

these six simple exercises we have all the basics we need to teach our hands the proper ways to achieve independence. Practice them slowly and with a metronome and don't move on to the next example until you've mastered the one before. With a little hard work and patience I think you'll see how valuable this lesson is.

WARMING UP

by Tony Franklin
February 1994

For a long time I played shows and wondered why it took me three or four tunes before I "got into it." How easy it is to overlook the obvious—warm-ups! So I started with the usual stuff (scales, arpeggios, etc.), which worked out very well. But I found it to be tedious (yes, I admit I can sometimes be lazy with practicing). So I devised a shortcut exercise that is so simple you may dismiss it. But try it first.

It consists of a short chromatic run, ascending and descending, using all four fingers of the fingering hand (Ex. 1). Play it in a continuous pattern, starting at a medium pace and gradually increasing speed.

Ex. 1

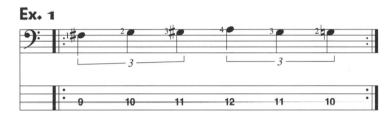

Start around the ninth fret and as you warm up move to the lower frets on the bottom string for the BIG stretch (Ex. 2). Be aware of keeping each note even and smooth, and pluck the strings aggressively to give both hands a warm-up. This is also a great strengthening exercise.

Ex. 2

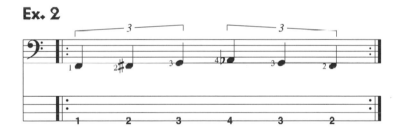

You'll be surprised. It doesn't sound like much, but it hurts and it works! Have fun!

GETTING (FRET)LESS OUT OF YOUR BASS

by Tony Franklin
March 1994

I always encourage players to try out the fretless bass—the richness of sound, the characteristic slides and the freedom of expression make all the extra effort worthwhile—oh, but that fretless sound sure is tempting… So fret not! There is hope. In my pre-fretless days I used various techniques on my fretted bass to achieve that much desired sound.

Ex. 1 is a short passage of music à la "A Remark You Made" from Weather Report's *Heavy Weather* album. Use it as a reference point to judge how your sound is changing as you modify the settings on your bass and make alterations to your playing style. Play it fairly slowly with much expression and pay special attention to the slides aiming to minimize any fret noise while still retaining enough "growl" to cut through. It's a process of listening and fine tuning according to your technique and your particular instrument.

Ex. 1

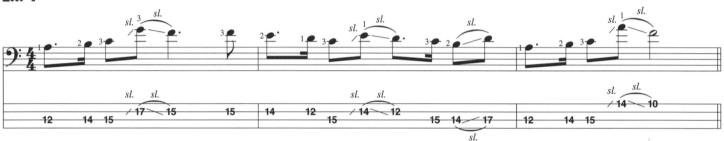

Play the melody in the example with your bass set up as you would normally use it. Then try these modifications:

- Switch to the bridge pickup (don't despair if you don't have one!).
- Experiment with the tone: cut the treble; boost the mids; boost the low end.
- If your bass has a single tone control, turn it about a quarter of the way around and fine tune it to find that sweet "honky" tone (this was the technique I used on my fretted Precision bass).
- Be sure to play fingerstyle, as a pick gives too much edge. For a "singing" fretless sound, gently pluck the strings, almost stroking them. The plucking hand should be positioned over the fingerboard, somewhere around the 20th fret.
- For a Jaco-type punchy sound, play really close to the bridge; using fingers, pluck the strings firmly (ouch!).
- Use a chorus pedal to fatten the sound, but not too much. For the big chorused sound, I suggest using two separate pedals.
- If you have a compressor or limiter, use this to enhance the fretless effect, especially for the "singing" sound.

Jaco Pastorius always encouraged fretted players to practice on the frets to promote accuracy and dexterity. I feel this is a good habit to incorporate, especially for those who are thinking of moving onto the fretless bass.

I enjoy the fretless bass, but of course my opinion is biased! It took quite a while, but if I can do it, so can you! Have fun…

GOING FOR A WALK

by Tony Franklin
May 1994

It's tried, it's tested, it's as old as the blues itself (well, almost!)—the good old walking bass line. Actually, its roots are more likely derived from jazz—those cats, never content to hold the root note for any longer than necessary (!), came up with something that's driving, grooving and exciting. Thanks boys, it's one of my favorites. So let's go for a walk!

The ideal vehicle for the walking bass line is the 12-bar blues. I've given a sample bass line that is typical of my approach (Ex. 1). Rather than using the standard I–IV–I–V–IV– I sequence, I've thrown in a few "extra" chords to spice it up a little. Play it with 12/8 shuffle feel, slowly at first, increasing speed as you gain confidence and familiarity. It'll work at any speed, though I had "fast" in mind for this particular example. I played a similar line to this on a track called "Texas Son" from Gary Hoey's album *Animal Instinct*—check it out.

I generally make it a rule of thumb to land on the root note on the downbeat of every chord change. I've made an exception to this at (a), so I've indicated the F9 chord in parentheses. I feel it's just about okay to be on the G note for the F9 chord but it's not a habit I encourage prolonged use of!

Ex. 1

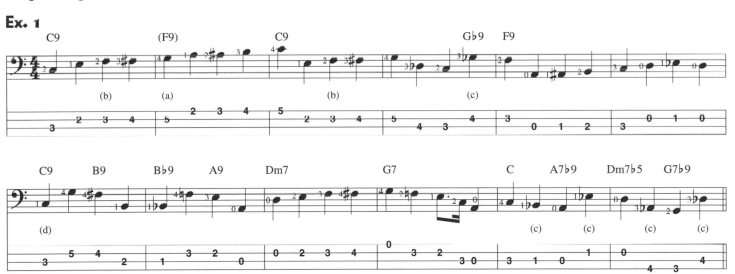

Ex. 2 shows an alternative way of getting to the F9 chord. It also shows the use of recurring patterns or phrases, which adds to the melodic content and gives a nice flow to the sequence. This recurring pattern also happens in Ex. 1 as indicated by (b).

Ex. 2

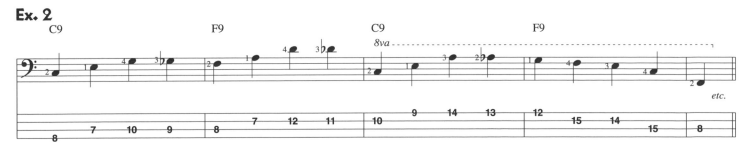

I like using these recurring phrases, especially over the first four measures, as I feel it gives an identity to the sequence and brings in a little "extra" to the (sometimes) overly tried-and-tested 12-bar riffs! This kind of pattern happens over the first four measures of Exs. 1 and 2. I've given two further examples of the same kind of thing (Exs. 3 and 4).

Ex. 3

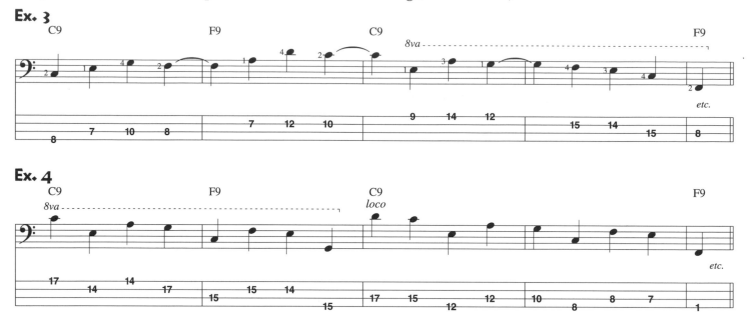

Ex. 4

Back to Ex. 1 at part (c): I like to resolve to a new chord change using a half-step drop. I guess this comes from my jazz days, but I feel it adds an ear-grabbing melodic twist and is quite atypical for rock and blues. I guess I'm just an atypical kind of guy—(Ha ha!)

Ex. 1 at part (d) is a descending chord sequence stretching over two measures. A variation of this section is given in Exs. 5a and 5b. Oh, the blues! An endless source of inspiration, and no shortage of variety.

Ex. 5A

Ex. 5B

As usual, I hope that these examples will spark off some of your own creative endeavors. Use them as a launching pad for some deep bass exploration!

One final point: I believe there should be humor in music. I like to do this by inserting a short passage of a familiar tune into an otherwise standard sequence. For instance, "Jingle Bells" fits very nicely into the blues sequence. It has to be done tastefully and subtly, and then people aren't sure if they heard it or not! I have a current favorite that I'm using but I won't tell you what it is—see if you can spot it if you see me play sometime. I'll be looking for you. Till then, keep smiling!

HARMONICS

by Tony Franklin
June 1994

Harmonics add an extra dimension to the bass player's range. I've been incorporating harmonics for some years now. They're captivating, fun and daring—just like me! (Hee hee!)

So, starting with the basics, use the bridge pickup and pluck the strings firmly, close to the bridge (if you don't have a bridge pickup, experiment with the tone control to find the "sweet spot"—about a third of the way 'round—to bring out the harmonics). There are harmonics all over the neck, but let's take a look between the third and fifth frets. Ex. 1 shows a scale using harmonics from this region of the neck. Notice the patterns that are formed with the finger positions as they move over the settings.

Ex. 1

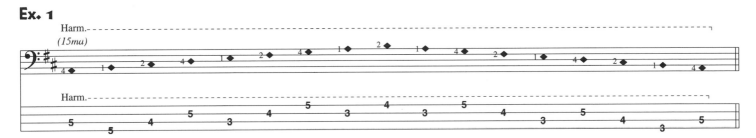

Jaco Pastorius inspired me to incorporate harmonic chords into my repertoire. It takes a bit of work to place them into songs (I'm still working on it!) but it's worth it, as they really grab the listener's ears.

Ex. 2 shows a few examples of harmonic chords (there are *many* more). I find them great for solo work, too. When using a two-or three-note harmonic chord, I let them ring and give the neck a tug (or a shake!) and it sounds like I've got a whammy bar!

Ex. 2

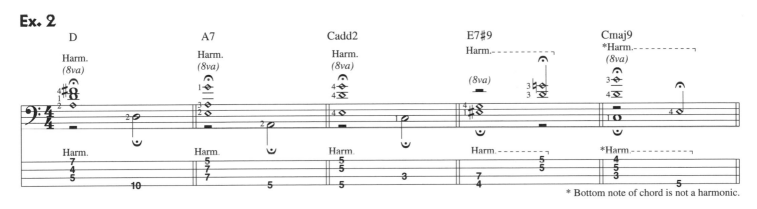

* Bottom note of chord is not a harmonic.

I love the way that Jaco used to strike a harmonics chord in a really unexpected place, letting it ring while the band went off into some musical mayhem exploration until Jaco pulled it back together by kicking into one of his smoking groove riffs. GOOD STUFF! I'm sure there is a place for this in today's rock music (I hope so). Jaco was a rocker and a musical rebel in many ways, and he's the king of harmonics; check out any record he did for evidence of that.

Ex. 3 shows a typical Jaco-type "explosion": you can re-enter with the groove at your leisure!

Ex. 3

Ex. 4 shows how to create a "false" harmonic. Holding down the B note on the A string (second fret) and striking a harmonic on the sixth fret creates a "false" D♯ harmonic. This is the same harmonic Jaco used on "Portrait of Tracy" that eluded me for so long. It's quite a stretch so I suggest trying it in a higher position to begin with.

Ex. 4

A few final tips:

- A compressor or sustainer helps the harmonics to ring longer.
- A chorus or harmonizer makes those harmonics sound so-o-o-o sweet.
- Plucking with the fingers (not a pick) makes them sound fatter and fuller.
- Harmonics are everywhere! Look for them all over the neck, especially on the lower frets.

Happy hunting!

THE SCIENCE OF HARMONICS

by Tony Franklin
July 1994

Okay, it's true, I've made reference to Jaco Pastorius more than a few times in these pages. He is without doubt my number-one bass influence, and the more I sit down and think about my "elements of style," I usually trace their roots back to Jaco.

For those players who are not familiar with his work, I highly recommend it. I'm not saying we all should start playing like Jaco but for those of us who seriously want to broaden our musical outlook (and not only bass players!), Jaco is certainly a significant piece of the jigsaw.

This next technique, which I've never really known what to call, is a Pastorius trademark. He described it as a purely mathematical process, which is why I called this month's column "The Science of Harmonics." Of course, Jaco was being totally modest about his playing when he described the technique this way; he omitted the necessity for dexterity, style and pure musical genius. These were qualities that Jaco took for granted in his playing.

The science of harmonics is similar to the "false" harmonics technique, but it goes a step (or two) further. False harmonics are made by holding down a note to create a temporary capo. From there we play a regular harmonic like you would on an open string (see Ex. 1). However, this is limited to the stretch of our fingering hand, and is only practical for isolated notes.

Ex. 1

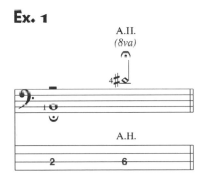

The science of harmonics (does this sound like a new-age dating service?!?) uses the picking hand to create the harmonic, allowing far more freedom for the fingering hand. (For the sake of convenience I shall refer to the plucking hand as the right hand, and the fingering hand as the left hand. Sorry, left-handers!)

- Choose a strong harmonic, e.g., the D harmonic on the seventh fret of the G string. Place the thumb of the right hand on the seventh-fret position and pluck the string with the index finger of the same hand to create the harmonic. It may seem a little alien at first, so experiment; try plucking with the nail; try plucking with the pad; try the middle finger; try another harmonic—see what works for you.

- With the left hand, play a C note on the fifth fret of the G string. Now, using the right-hand harmonic method as previously described, strike a harmonic on the 17th fret of the G string (see Ex. 2). This will create an octave harmonic to the C on the fifth fret. Following along with Ex. 3, work your way up the fingerboard, holding down the note with the left hand and striking the corresponding octave harmonic with the right-hand. Keep going all the way off the fingerboard with the right hand, using your eye and your ear to pick out the octave harmonics. Remember, the higher the register the less the physical distance between the notes on the string.

Ex. 2

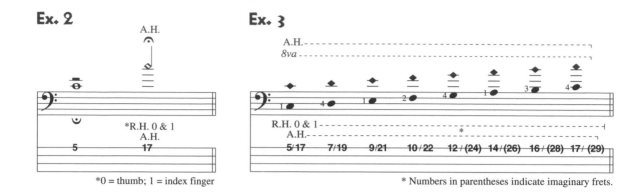

*0 = thumb; 1 = index finger

* Numbers in parentheses indicate imaginary frets.

Of course, when we're off the fingerboard in this way, we have no fret markers to guide us. So, to make this technique usable in performance, we need to identify our own reference points on the body of the bass. It could be a scratch, a screw, a pickup or a battle scar. It's a personal thing, so start looking!

The mathematics of the technique come from subdividing the distance between the left-hand note and the bridge. Simple, ay? Sure!!

Jaco makes it sound so easy, especially on the intro to "Birdland" from Weather Report's *Heavy Weather*. He even uses the double octave harmonic in this passage, which can be found using the same technique in the upper reaches of the strings (about three inches from the bridge).

Ex. 4 is a little tune that's designed to develop your skills in the science of harmonics. It works at any speed. It isn't possible to give the right-hand fret positions as they're off the fingerboard. They're always an octave higher than the written note—unless you want to try for the double octave! Go for it!

Ex. 4

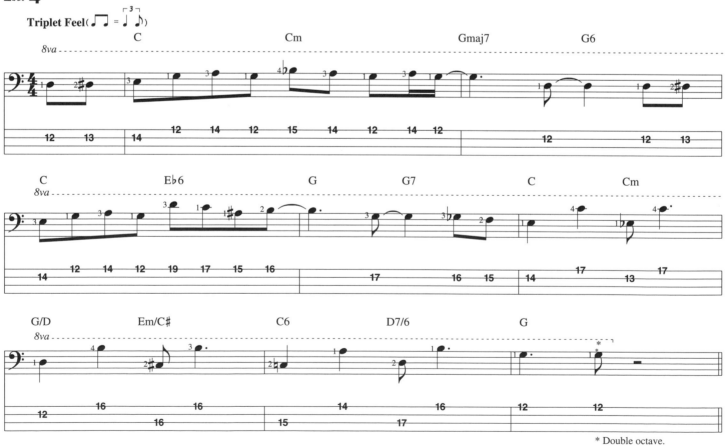

* Double octave.

Be patient and have fun!

SLIDING HARMONICS

by Tony Franklin
August 1994

This technique is exclusive to the fretless bass. (I'm not wishing to exclude the fretted guys'n'gals; rather, I would hope to inspire you to venture into fretless land—a recurring theme in these pages, I believe.)

"Sliding harmonics" is a technique that, for once, is NOT a Jaco Pastorius trademark! I first heard it on Paul Young's "Wherever I Lay My Hat," which features the extraordinary fretless talents of Mr. Pino Palladino. I really wanted to use the technique but didn't know how to do it, and to be totally honest, I have no idea how I learned it! But somehow it came to me and I'm glad it did, for I've used it extensively since then.

After "What was it like to play with Jimmy Page?" the question I'm most frequently asked is "How do you slide harmonics?" So here's my answer!

- Choose a strong harmonic, e.g., the D harmonic on the seventh fret of the G string. Immediately after plucking the string (good and firmly), hold down the string on the seventh-fret position. The harmonic will still ring. (Remember, on the fretless bass, we play on the fret—or where the fret would be—so if you're trying this on a fretted bass, you'll need to hold the string down on the fret as well.)

- Holding down the string with the harmonic ringing, slide up to the 12th fret. See Ex. 1. The harmonic should slide, too. Keep trying if it doesn't.

- Try it with different harmonics and different strings, sliding up and down. It's a simple technique, but so very effective. Indeed, the very first time I was heard in this country (U.S.A.), the song featured the infamous "sliding harmonicus." I'm referring, of course, to the introduction of the Firm's "Radioactive." See Ex. 2 for an exercise similar to the "Radioactive" lick. Another instance can be found on "You've Lost That Lovin' Feeling" from the same eponymous Firm album.

Ex. 1

Ex. 2

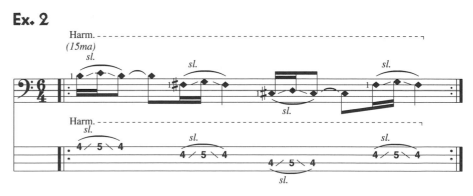

As far as the other question goes: Mr. Page is a scholar, a gentleman and a musical master craftsman, and he's also a crazy Englishman like me! Thanks, Jimmy, and thanks to all of you for listening. I'll see you later. Byeee!

A BREAK FROM THE EIGHTH

by Tony Franklin
September 1994

I can remember being in bands—writing, exploring, learning; maybe we'd start with a guitar riff or a drum groove or a vocal melody. Whatever it was, when it came to the bass part, and especially in the context of rock music, the most appropriate line would be the eighth-note pump.

I played it, of course, but secretly I'd be complaining, "Why does everyone else get the interesting parts and I—once again!—get stuck with *dum-dum-dum-dum-dum-dum-dum-dum?!*" But let's face it, sometimes it is the most appropriate thing to do for the riff, the groove, and the song. I guess it's a bass player's lot! But I still was brooding, and over the years I experimented with pushing the boundaries of the eighth-note pump. Here are some of the results of my explorations.

Ex. 1 accentuates the eighth-note offbeat. We can take this a step further by omitting the downbeats, as in Ex. 2. This is a favorite of mine. An example would be to use the offbeat feel in a verse or a bridge section and then double up for the chorus.

Ex. 1

Ex. 2

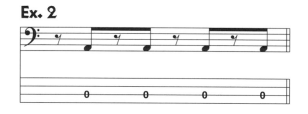

Ex. 3 has different accents, and these should not be overly pronounced. It's a Latin-ish kind of feel which when used in a rock context, with a straight drum pattern, creates an undulating-pulse feel. Notice that the accented notes are played on the fifth fret, while the unaccented notes are played on the open string (try it the other way 'round, too). This creates a subtle change of tone on the accents. Don't be afraid to let the open string ring, but use your judgment and do what's appropriate for the song—be a good listener. (I find this rule applies to many areas of my life besides music!) This open-note/fingered-note technique also can be applied to Ex. 1.

Ex. 3

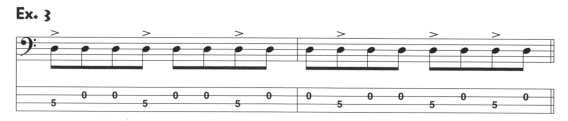

Ex. 4 takes the Latin feel a little further—maybe too far—but I always think we should take things to the outer limits because you never know what you might discover (use your discretion). If we always play safe, we often can limit ourselves. So go for it!

Ex. 4

Ex. 5 and 6 are hip-hop-ish. This is another one of my favorite styles. These examples work best with a drummer or drum machine. Start with a straight pattern (à la "Billie Jean") and notice how these patterns feel like they turn the beat around. You'll see what I mean when you try them. When you're more comfortable with them, have some fun with the drummer (you can't do this with a drum machine!): turn the beat around, drop beats, create counter-rhythms, go to the edge. This is also an exercise in counting. (Where's "one"?!)

Ex. 5

Ex. 6

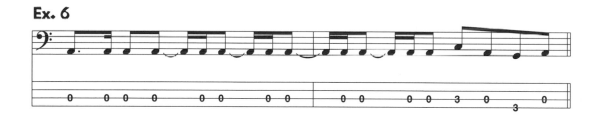

So there we have it. There's many more examples, of course, but I'll leave you to make your own discoveries. Happy hunting!

PLAYING BEHIND THE BEAT

by Tony Franklin
October 1994

Playing behind the beat. What does this mean? Playing out of time? Slowing up? Holding back? Well, yes—but not really! It's an interesting subject, one that isn't easy to define. However, it is an important aspect of my style and approach, so I'll try to convey something of its concept to you. "Playing behind" is inherent in most British rock bands and is especially apparent in the works of Led Zeppelin. We only have to recall the lurching sway of "Since I've Been Loving You" to get an idea of what we're talking about. Ex. 1 is based on a two-bar excerpt from "Since I've Been Loving You," and finds Led Zep in full "lurch" mode. The chord sequence shown is heard throughout the song, but these measures are like the ones before the guitar solo. The first of the two measures is especially important for the bass as there's just one note played per beat (the time signature is 12/8, which means $\downarrow$. = one beat), so absolutely no rushing allowed! If in doubt, hold back!

Ex. 1

In complete contrast to "Since…" are the sizzling salsa rhythms of Latin America. If the English beat is pulling back, then the Latin beat is definitely pushing forward. It's inherent in the cultures of these countries: the Latinos being the more urgent, go-get-up-and-dance type, while the English are more laid-back than is sometimes good for them (myself included). So it's natural to expect these aspects to reflect in the music of these countries. Now, being English myself, I have a certain understanding of playing behind the beat. But despite its being inherent in the music of my country, I was not born with the ability to play this way. I had to learn the skill, and the process almost lost me my gig at the time! The drummer in the band brought to my attention the importance of the bass player keeping time (as well as the drummer!) and how the rhythm section should pull together. This may sound painfully obvious, but I still hear players who seem like they're playing for themselves and not with each other as a unit. The rhythm section is the foundation of the band and we cannot build a strong house on a shaky foundation. It was a lesson for me to be more aware and to listen—so simple yet so important.

But like many other things we do, we don't even know we're doing them until somebody points it out to us (which can be painful); and the American way of life being the way it is—very fast and achievement-oriented—I'm sure there's more than a few of us who could benefit from being more relaxed and "behind the beat" in more areas than just music.

Did I swim too far out from the shore? Bear with me!

I usually give a music example to illustrate the point I'm explaining, but this isn't as obvious a subject as usual. Try this . . . Ex. 2 is a straight eighth-note pattern. Play it alongside a basic drum pattern (à la "Billie Jean" but slower, at about 85 b.p.m.) and alternate between pushing the feel and laying back. See if you can feel the difference. It's easier to put it down on tape and listen back afterwards, and it's definitely better to use a drum machine in the beginning.

Ex. 2

When it comes to practical application in a band, it largely depends on the interaction and communication between the bass player and the drummer. Have a listen to "Since I've Been Loving You" again, and also "When the Levee Breaks" and any number of classic Led Zep tunes. As a comparison, check out The Police's "Every Little Thing She Does Is Magic" or "Driven to Tears" to get an idea of pushing or "being on top" of the beat. The reggae overtones of The Police are definitely more pushy—but it works, and I'm a big Sting and Police fan.

There are so many options and varieties in music (thank goodness!), and at the end of the day, we have to choose what works best for us. The Golden Rule? It has to *feel good!*

Well, I hope you get something from this. It's been an interesting journey for me. Thanks for listening. Take care and God bless.

~~~~

STAMINA

by Tony Franklin
November 1994

I recently read an article on Jaco Pastorius where various musicians who'd known him and played with him were commenting and reminiscing about their friend, the master of the electric fretless bass. I noticed that a recurring theme was Jaco's stamina. His bass lines undoubtedly were more demanding than most, both physically and mentally; nonetheless, stamina is an important aspect for all bass players.

I always encourage playing fingerstyle instead of with the pick because of the noticeable difference in tone and versatility. Fingerstyle is more of a workout, especially over the duration of a gig, and especially if you're like me and prefer to play hard. I've also noticed that when it comes to gig time, I seem to play 10 times harder and my forearms feel like they're going to explode, no matter how much rehearsal time I've had. What's the cure? Keep gigging, I suppose; but this isn't always possible, so we'll try plan B. I've devised some shortcut strengthening exercises that hurt but work! Here's a few of them.

Ex. 1a is a straightforward octave pattern. All these patterns should be played as quickly as you are able while still keeping the left and right hands in sync. Pluck the string firmly and close to the bridge for maximum benefit. If you are able to make the octave stretch with the third finger instead of the fourth, then do so. In fact, try playing the exercise an octave higher using the third finger. Also try playing the octaves with the second and fourth fingers. Ex. 1b is a variation using a paradiddle-type rhythm pattern. Ex. 1c is another rhythmic variation. Look for some of your own, too. For a bigger stretch, do the above exercises with a 10th interval, as in Ex. 1d. If you play a five- or six-string bass, you can make a bigger interval jump from the top to bottom strings.

Ex. 1A

Ex. 1B

Ex. 1C

Ex. 1D

Ex. 2a is a pattern similar to a riff I played on "Riptide" from Gary Hoey's soundtrack album *The Endless Summer II*. Make a loop of this and the following patterns, keeping the left and right hands in sync and maintaining evenness with each note. Ex. 2b and 2c are more variations that work specifically on the ring finger and pinkie.

Ex. 2A

Ex. 2B

Ex. 2C

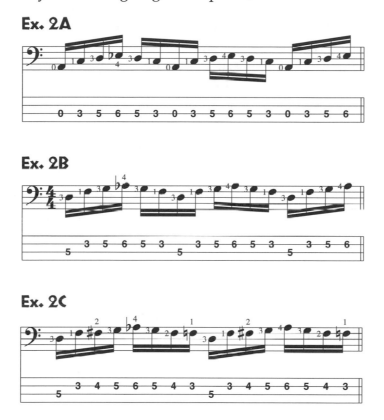

Ex. 3 is a Jaco favorite, the 6th-interval scale, which also helps develop dexterity.

Ex. 3

Ex. 4 is based on the up-tempo solo section from Led Zep's "Dazed and Confused," which always got me gritting my teeth. For an all-round workout, alternate the fingering between fingers 1 and 3 (as written) and 2 and 4.

Ex. 4

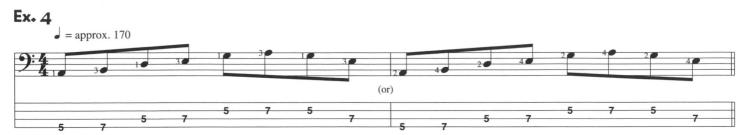

When I think of stamina, I naturally associate it with physical fitness. My own experiences have shown me that I am a better all-round performer when I'm in shape. I've seen both sides of the coin. During my days with The Firm and Blue Murder I was *not* in shape. In fact, I was doing everything I could to be out of shape! Still, I attained a certain degree of success, but I now believe that any success achieved while out of control is ultimately short-lived. Then there's the other side of the argument: Would Jimi Hendrix be the legend he is if he'd been a drug-free, jogging vegetarian? I don't think so! It's all about timing, the age we live in and personal evolution. Myself, I'm happy to be healthier now, as I feel more equipped to face the rigors of life as well as the hurdles of the music industry.

For maintaining musical stamina there's not substitute for playing and jamming. When I'm not gigging or recording, I regularly get together with my drummer to jam—or I use a drum machine. I make grooves from the exercises in this article. I deliberately play a little harder, but not too much. Trust me, I've found out—the hard way—the value of staying in shape between gigs. It's necessary to rest but you just never know when that big break is coming; the all-important audition, which often arrives at a moment's notice. I blew a really important audition some years back because I was out of shape, and believe me, that hurt far more than my forearms did! Don't let it happen to you. Get strong and stay strong!

Thanks for listening. I'll see you in the gym!

11THS AND 13THS

by Tony Franklin
December 1994

I discovered a nice little exercise the other day that also sounds good. It's simple yet effective and is based on the 11th and 13th arpeggios. There are basically two forms of each arpeggio, the minor and the major (see Ex. 1a and 1b). When you play them side by side you can hear the difference between the two, the first being the major 11th arpeggio and the second the minor 11th. I like them because I can cover a lot of ground without too much movement, which I feel is an important aspect of bass playing (let's make it easy on ourselves!).

Ex. 1A

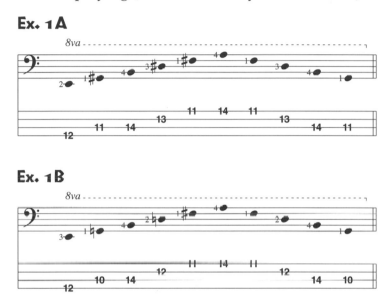

Ex. 1B

These are deceptive little exercises; like tongue twisters, the individual elements are simple, but put them all together and they get tricky! I discovered this a few nights ago when playing a gig with my old mate Gary Hoey. With his music being all instrumental, I got to have a good ol' play, with a few bass solos here and there. During a solo I remembered the minor 11th arpeggio and thought I'd slip it in. but my tongue-tied fingers became thoroughly twisted! The real key to these arpeggios is the fingering, especially the starting note. Of course, the fingering differs between the minor and major arpeggios.

For the sake of these exercises try to keep each note even, with a nice flow. As you become more fluent, you can juggle them and pull them about rhythmically. They are especially useful for soloing or filling. They very subtly (usually!) and sweetly take the emphasis away from the root note, which is something I enjoy doing.

Ex. 2a and 2b take it a stage further by adding the 13th, which also means we have to move around the fingerboard some more. Once you've remembered the basic shapes of these arpeggios, try them in different positions on the neck, especially lower down for the BIG stretch; don't get stuck in one area, keep flexible.

Ex. 2A

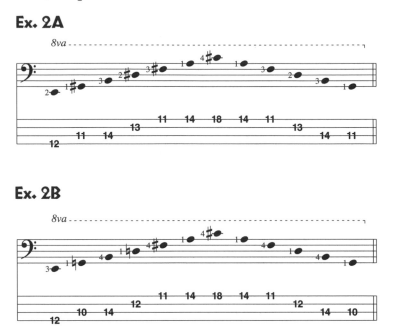

Ex. 2B

The purpose of these exercises is multifold. They get you stretching in many ways: they strengthen the fingers; they get you moving around the fingerboard; they stretch our musical imaginations by challenging us to find the right context in which to use them. They're not obvious riffs by any means, but I find them so pretty and so musical that I want to find places to use them. Also, we don't necessarily have to use the whole arpeggio.

These exercises will introduce you to areas you possibly haven't ventured into before, and I always say we need to build up our musical libraries (by listening, experimenting, etc.) so we have a greater variety of influences and perspectives to draw upon when it comes to creating our own musical expressions (Frank Zappa's main influences were the blues and Stravinsky!). Remember, the idea is to keep flexible.

STRETCHING THE BOUNDARIES, PART 1

by Tony Franklin
January 1995

This month I want to talk about detuning the bass, a technique I've been using for many years. It most commonly occurs on the low E string, usually down to D. But there are other tunings, as we'll come to see.

I first became aware of the option to detune when I heard "White Man" by Queen from *A Day at the Races* in 1976. It blew my impressionable mind and opened up whole new vistas of exploration. Having since worked with such greats as Jimmy Page and Roy Harper, I've discovered that detuning—or retuning—has been around for a long time. Its roots stem from the blues: the open-chord tunings were perfect for the slice and one-finger barre chords, allowing the early bluesmen's feelings to flow freely without the distraction of the technical aspects of playing guitar.

Folk music took it a stage further by tailoring the guitar's tuning to whatever the song or mood required. Jimmy Page said if the guitar didn't have the note he wanted, he'd retune it to give him what he needed. Led Zeppelin, in my opinion, were at the pinnacle of alternate guitar tunings: they provided us, as did folk music, with many varieties of open tunings, each requiring different playing skills and producing unique chord voicings.

Meanwhile, on the bass, which as a rule doesn't play more than one note at a time, alternate tunings may seem a little redundant. Let's go on a journey…

One of my earliest (obvious) alternate tunings was the low D on The Firm's "Midnight Moonlight," from the band's first album. The song is in D and so it seemed natural for me to drop to the low D; this is something I still do. A certain mental adjustment is needed when we change tunings, but I find this is easily overcome by associating the piece of music with the new tuning. Any fingering and positioning can change because of part of that song's character and identity.

One of the advantages of the low-D tuning is that when we play the low E (on the second fret of the detuned low string), we can get a much sweeter tone (especially on the fretless) than the regular open E string. We also can add vibrato, or slide up to the note (very effective on ballads).

Another perk of low-D tuning is the natural octave it creates with the regular open D string. This allows us to play octaves with greater flexibility and accuracy (which is especially useful on the fretless!). I use the second and third fingers on the fingering hand (see Ex. 1), and depending on the style of the piece of music, I'll often damp the open A and G strings with the sides of those same fingers (try it—it's easier to do than to explain!). For instance, if I'm playing aggressively with a pick (this is one of the rare occasions that I do!), I'll use this "smoother" technique. Visually this is very exciting, too, as we can "strum" all four strings like a guitar, leaving only the octave to ring out. You may want to try it with different combinations of fingerings; see what works best for you. I had to develop some new calluses, too, so watch out!

Ex. 1

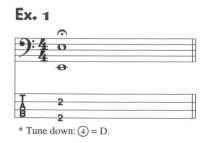

* Tune down: ④ = D.

I used this technique to great effect on the solo section of "Valley of the Kings" from Blue Murder's first album. Ex. 2 is an exercise similar to that passage. Note that it was played on the fretless bass, so the slides are grandiose and deliberate. I tell you, those octave slides on the fretless sound huge! It's much more effective than an octave pedal, because there's always a slight intonation difference between the upper and lower strings, and a variation of tone as well. (This also occurs on the fretted bass.) I'm biased towards the fretless bass (as if you couldn't tell!), which is why I take every opportunity to encourage folks to try it. Sure, it's a challenge, but it's so much FUN! I promise you.

Ex. 2

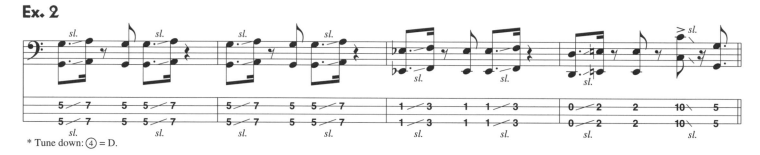

* Tune down: ④ = D.

When playing the octave D's, it's difficult to strike the two notes simultaneously with any amount of power. But no worry! We can create a "chase and follow" delivery—effective when sliding the octaves—by playing the low note first, then playing the octave an eighth note later, or whatever is appropriate for the rhythm of the song. I used this style of playing on Gary Hoey's tune "Blast" from his *Endless Summer II* soundtrack. Check out the B-section of that song to see what I mean.

Try playing some of your favorite bass lines, or even top-line melodies, in octaves using the low-D technique. Experiment with fingers and the pick. It gets you moving about because essentially it's a one-string exercise. One of my favorite lines is Stevie Wonder's "I Wish" (play it in D). Try the national anthem top line, or whatever appeals to you. Have fun and watch out for those calluses!

STRETCHING THE BOUNDARIES, PART 2

by Tony Franklin
February 1995

In "Stretching the Boundaries, Part I" I talked about alternate tunings, especially the low D tuning and the natural octave it creates with the regular open D string. I'm going to continue right where I left off…

We can take this open-octave tuning a stage further by detuning the A string to G, forming an octave with the regular open G string. Or tune the regular G string up to an A, forming an octave with the regular open A string. There are many variations. For instance, I once met a guy who tuned all the strings down a whole step (the rest of the band was in regular tuning) because he liked the deeper tone he got from the bass. It also allowed him to play the roots of common guitar keys like A, E, D, and G (common because of the convenience of open strings) as fingered notes, which gave him sweeter tone flexibility, as I mentioned in the previous issue.

I often find that these and other tunings are useful in songwriting because they make us adapt. We have to think and play differently as they present us with a new sound palette to paint with, which brings out different aspects of ourselves. It's like sitting at a piano, or trying an instrument other than our own, or picking up an instrument we haven't played for some time. I find that the instrument and the new sounds we hear (or the once-familiar ones seen in a different light) spark off something within us; they inspire us to create something new. It's very exciting because we get beyond ourselves and just let the magic of the moment take over. The art is not to be in the way of the process. Don't think about it, just do it!

Jimmy Page used to change his guitar tunings according to the requirements of a particular song. It didn't matter if the tuning was traditional or otherwise; if the piece called for it, then it had to be so. This thinking inspired my playing on a song called "Billy" from Blue Murder's first album. The riff is a fast-moving, descending E–D–B pattern, and I was having problems landing cleanly on the B. So I moved the A string up a step to give myself an open B and ended the problem. It sounds simple, I know, but I get asked about this quite often.

Now, with the recent popularity of five- and six-string basses (which have been around longer than you may think), lower notes and greater range are more readily available to us bass players. I have to say that I've never been drawn to the five-string; maybe I'm just too traditional (or is that a polite way of saying *stubborn?!*). When Jaco Pastroius was asked about the five-string bass, he would reply simply, "What for?" He felt that the regular electric bass had everything it ever needed and that the dynamic range and style came from the hand and imagination of the player. I feel the same way to a certain degree, but also, I've never gotten along with the spacing of the strings on a five- or six-string bass because of the way I play. But that's just me! Thank goodness we're all different, because this world would be a dull place otherwise!

Here's some food for thought. The electric bass is modeled after the upright bass, with the same E, A, D, G tuning. But the electric bass is just as closely related to the cello, which has C, G, D, A tuning. It would be interesting to tune the bass like the cello (with different string gauges), as we'd immediately have a far greater range, comparable to the five-string. Does this sound appealing or appalling? I guess *I'll* have to try it!

What I'm essentially saying is that we shouldn't limited ourselves by sticking with the familiar just because everyone else does it. I think it was King Louis XIV who requested that his wife lay down so he could see his child being born, and since then almost everybody does it that way. It happens to be a very unnatural way to give birth, but that's how traditions start, by somebody doing it first and others following suit.

We can start our own new traditions by breaking from the norm, trusting and following our hearts and instincts. Go on, stretch your boundaries; you'll be surprised how much you can do.

Thanks for listening.

~~~

• BASS TABLATURE EXPLANATION/NOTATION LEGEND •

Bass tablature is a four-line staff that graphically represents the bass fingerboard. By placing a number on the appropriate line, the string and fret of any note can be indicated. The number 0 represents an open string. For example:

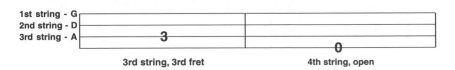

1st string - G
2nd string - D
3rd string - A

3rd string, 3rd fret   4th string, open

Definitions for Special Bass Notation (for both traditional and tablature bass lines)

BEND: Strike the note and bend up 1/2 step (one fret).

BEND: Strike the note and bend up a whole step (two frets).

BEND AND RELEASE: Strike the note. Bend up 1/2 (or whole) step, then release the bend back to the original note. All three notes are tied; only the first note is struck.

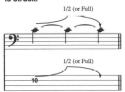

PRE-BEND: Bend the note up 1/2 (or whole) step, then strike it.

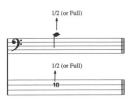

PRE-BEND AND RELEASE: Bend the note up 1/2 (or whole) step. Strike it and release the bend back to the original note.

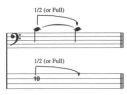

VIBRATO: Vibrate the note by rapidly bending and releasing it with the left hand.

SLIDE: Strike the first note and then with the same left-hand finger move up the string to the location of the second note. The second note is not struck.

SLIDE: Same as above, except the second note is struck.

SLIDE: Slide up to the note indicated from a few frets below.

SLIDE: Strike the note and slide up an indefinite number of frets, releasing finger pressure at the end of the slide.

HAMMER-ON: Strike the first (lower) note, then sound the higher note with another finger by fretting it without picking.

4th string - E

PULL-OFF: Place both fingers on the notes to be sounded. Strike the first (higher) note, then sound the lower note by pulling the finger off the higher note while keeping the lower note fretted.

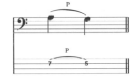

TAPPING: Hammer ("tap") the fret indicated with the right-hand index or middle finger and pull off to the note fretted by the left hand ("T" indicates "tapped" notes).

NATURAL HARMONIC: With a left-hand finger, lightly touch the string over the fret indicated, then strike it. A chime-like sound is produced.

ARTIFICIAL HARMONIC: Fret the note normally and sound the harmonic by lightly touching the node point on the string with the edge of the right-hand thumb while simultaneously plucking with the right-hand index or middle finger.

PALM MUTE: If using a pick, partially mute the note by lightly touching the string with the right hand just before the bridge.

SLAP AND POP: Slap (▼) the string with the side of the thumb. Pop (○) or snap the string with the index or middle finger by pulling and releasing it so that it rebounds against the fretboard.

MUFFLED STRING: Lay the left hand across the string without depressing it to the fretboard. Strike the string with the right hand, producing a percussive sound.

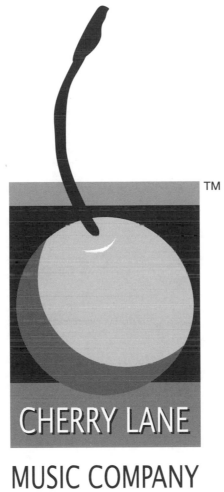

TM

CHERRY LANE

MUSIC COMPANY

QUALITY IN PRINTED MUSIC